Five Marys

FAMILY STYLE

RECIPES AND TRADITIONS FROM THE RANCH

MARY HEFFERNAN

with Jess Thomson

PHOTOGRAPHY BY ERIN KUNKEL

FOR MY PARENTS, who started the traditions I love most

Contents

SPRING

SUMMER

Our Family, Traditions, and Recipes

I ALWAYS KNEW I WANTED A BIG FAMILY. I grew up the oldest of four in Menlo Park, California, in a close family that has been in the state for six generations, many of them in agriculture. The four of us understood from a young age that family comes first, and between holidays and reunions, we spent lots of time with aunts, uncles, and grandparents. My parents were each one of five, so that made for a lot of cousins, and growing up, I loved every part of it—the chaos, the huge gatherings, the constant celebration.

Food was always the centerpiece of our get-togethers. I used to help my dad shop for our family's ravioli (page 267), and I remember going to get crab with him every year around Christmas (see page 67). My favorite dinner of my mom's was lamb chops with broccoli, and my dad made amazing tri-tip on the grill. As I got older, I knew that making and sharing meals with family would also be a cornerstone of my adult life. When I met my husband, Brian, a fifth-generation Californian who grew up on an almond farm, I knew I'd found my partner. He had a combination of intelligence and down-to-earth brawn that drew me right in the moment we met. And he was raised in a big, devoted family that valued togetherness above all else too. Part of what made us a great match was that we held similar priorities for our own future family and wanted our children to grow up with the same reverence for food, and specifically for family meals.

Before long, we had established a settled (if busy) life together, with four girls ages five and under in our storybook Craftsman house in a suburban neighborhood close to where I grew up. Brian worked as a corporate lawyer, but he and I also owned a few farm-to-table restaurants in the Bay Area. We learned that we loved working side by side despite the demands of the restaurants. We wanted to offer our customers delicious meat that was raised well. We hunted down small-scale operations that were focused on good genetics and great marbling and were frustrated by how little we found. When we couldn't find a small farm who could supply us with great beef year-round, we decided to do it ourselves.

Brian and I had always wanted to find property for family adventures and to escape from the busyness of the Bay Area, but the timing had never been right. In 2013, we started searching in earnest for land where we could raise livestock. The original plan was to hire ranch help and begin raising beef for our restaurants, traveling back and forth on weekends—another business, but not necessarily another life. We still laugh at ourselves for thinking we could fit ranch work into a weekend. When we found the historic Sharps Gulch Ranch in Fort Jones, California (population: 689), we saw so much potential: There were 1,800 acres of gorgeous land—a combination of pasture along a river valley and well-forested hills for grazing. The smaller of the two houses on the property was going to be easier to fix up quickly; it needed work but wouldn't be as much of an undertaking as restoring the large old homestead. We relished the idea of living smaller and knew that the small house, which we began to call the Little House, would work for us with our girls. The community was kind and welcoming. We couldn't wait to show our girls a different, more rural life. And believe it or not, driving six hours each way to and from the Bay Area with four kids seemed totally doable. We bought the ranch in December 2013 and became only its third owners in 160 years.

For the first two months, we went up every weekend and jumped into ranching without knowing much about what we were doing. Most people thought our plan was outrageous, but the more time we spent at the ranch, the more it felt like our true home. Other ranchers we met were very generous with help and advice. The girls happily shared one double bed, just as I had done with my siblings for years while my parents renovated our childhood home. And returning to Menlo Park after spending the weekend in the Little House felt like leaving the place we loved the most. It didn't take long before Brian and I looked at each other and made the huge decision to become full-time ranchers. After Francie finished

kindergarten in June 2014, we moved north to the ranch for good and began a new life raising animals for meat. It was actually the easiest decision we've ever made. Stepping out of the truck onto the ranch that day, knowing we didn't have to get back in, felt so right.

When we started ranching, we knew we wanted to raise cattle for beef; I had to talk Brian into adding pigs and sheep to our operation. We were lucky to have a mentor in Brian's brother-in-law, a rancher from Eastern Oregon, who advised us as we were starting up (and still answers plenty of late-night calls). While Brian started refining our breeding and feeding programs, I focused on sales and marketing. We also made a few big decisions about how we wanted to care for our animals. We learned a lot about doctoring and decided we would not harvest animals that had received antibiotics for our meat program. (We also never, ever withhold medicine when an animal needs it.) We dedicated ourselves to bottle-feeding young calves or lambs that didn't get enough milk from their mothers, growing our herd with high-quality genetics in our breeding stock, calving each fall, and shipping our meat directly to our customers. We don't do anything unless we're proud of it, and from a ranching perspective, that means giving our animals the very best care every single day, from birth to butchery.

The other big part of our ranch life is our restaurant. In the 1850s, the old building we call Five Marys Burgerhouse, which is about five minutes from the ranch, was opened as the town bar. It has always been the local watering hole and a cornerstone of the Fort Jones community. When it went up for sale in 2017, we tried to talk ourselves out of buying it every way we could, but somehow we found out that the then-owners were distant relatives with a great-great-grandmother also named Mary Heffernan, from the same tiny Irish village Brian's family came from seven generations back. We knew well how hard it is to run a restaurant, but it seemed too serendipitous to pass up! We wanted the Burgerhouse to be a gathering place where we could share our ranch-raised meats with our community. We like to say the Burgerhouse has good food, good drinks, and great people, because that's what it's really all about.

In 2021, we opened Five Marys Custom Meat Co., a craft butchery just down the road from the ranch. Building our own meat-cutting facility with state-of-the-art equipment and dry-aging rooms has given us total control over how we want each animal broken down. We've honed the size of every steak we cut, the smokiness of our bacon, the spiciness of our sausage, and the aging process of our beef to our exact specifications. This latest evolution of our business lets us fully realize our mission of supplying customers with high-quality, well-raised meat.

While we may have control over how we run our business, days on the ranch are full of compromise. Ranching requires a willing attitude toward early mornings, hours of chores, constant animal emergencies, and inclement weather. Our life doesn't really have quiet seasons. Even on the days when the restaurant is closed and we aren't shipping meat, animal care is our top priority and never stops—both morning and evening, we don't eat until all our animals have eaten first. Brian gets up at 4:45 a.m. every day, often to get hit by whatever emergency has come up overnight, but he still says his worst days ranching are better than his best days lawyering. He coined a family motto that we all work to live by: Be kind. Don't whine. Be tough. The girls have learned so much about grit and perseverance, and they've grown into strong, confident, competent contributors, helping out with almost every aspect of our operation. Living on a ranch might mean tromping off to the barn before dawn in a rainstorm to help a momma pig give birth, but having a common purpose—making the ranch run together, as a family—makes all the difficult and uncomfortable times worthwhile. The girls face challenges that bring them together to strategize, brainstorm, and cooperate, so that by dusk, when we sit down to eat together, they share a common sense of achievement.

Our evening meals as a family give us a chance to reflect on each day, talk about what went well or what we might do differently, and enjoy the meat we work so hard to raise. We plant a giant garden every spring, so in the summer and fall we always have plenty of homegrown produce too. Except in winter, we often cook and eat outdoors, enjoying the ranch's natural landscape together from Camp, our outdoor kitchen on a big hill (see page 157), sometimes with friends and neighbors. And continuing our upbringings, Brian and I spend as much time as possible with our family—both with our immediate family and extended family from near and far. There are cousin campouts on our land and meetups at rodeos and of course the yearly holiday rituals, both at my parents' house and with Brian's family. No matter where we are, any gathering means an excuse to make good food.

In my first book, *Five Marys Ranch Raised Cookbook*, I focused on individual recipes, including some of our family's favorite ways to prepare our beef, pork, and lamb. In these pages, you'll find some of our family's longtime favorite meals and traditions, divided by season into entire menus you can re-create at home. There's everything from the prime rib feast (page 71) we make on Christmas Eve at my parents' house in Menlo Park to my great-grandmother's famous homemade ravioli (page 267). You'll find the birthday meal (page 231) my girls request every year without fail and the beef pasties (page 217) we pack for rodeo competition lunches. While the recipes vary in seasonality and preparation time, they're all great options for feeding a crowd. To me, the menus feel festive without being fussy, and because our celebrations often revolve around all-day projects like branding and sheep-shearing, there are a few menus you can make almost entirely ahead of time. (You don't have to be branding to enjoy our Branding Day Dinner [page 249], but a Long Day Manhattan [page 252] really does taste best after a long day!)

Of course, from the menus, you can pick out recipes to come back to again and again, regardless of whether you're entertaining friends or just getting everyone fed on a busy weeknight. At the top of my list: the Double-Beef Chili with Black Beans and Sweet Potatoes (page 131) I make nonstop when the mercury drops;

delicious Camp Carnitas Tacos (page 146) we rely on when we have a crowd to feed; and Grilled Steaks with Chermoula Butter (page 299) that turn a simple backyard barbecue into a real party.

This is the food that Brian and I love, but it's also food my kids love. In our family, the girls do some of the cooking, so I've included a few of their favorites as well as the stories and traditions that surround our meals. Wherever I can, I include instructions for making things in advance, because feeding a family doesn't always coincide with free time just before the dinner bell. You'll also find fun DIY (do-it-yourself) projects and crafts that can be done alone or as a group—things like hand-rolling beeswax candles (page 99) or using real indigo dye to make *shibori*-style hand towels (page 207). (If you need to know how to make a campfire [page 189] or tether a horse [page 308], I've got you covered there too.)

Much like raising livestock, creating a cookbook is a labor of love. I've so enjoyed compiling our family's traditions and some new favorite recipes in this book for you. I hope you find comforting, deeply flavorful food that's nice enough to slow down for, but casual enough to enjoy any night of the week. When our work is done on the ranch, we enjoy the food our land provides, mostly outside, always together. I hope that sharing our family's experiences, recipes, and traditions inspires you to create your own. And I hope that as you start your day and face challenges—or the "always somethings" come up no matter where you live—you remember our family motto: Be kind. Don't whine. Be tough. And then kick your feet up and enjoy a hearty meal and a well-earned drink at the end of the day.

Francie

Janie

Maisie

Tessa

OUR GIRLS

When our first daughter was born, we knew we wanted to name her Mary, because both Brian and I come from Catholic families and have multiple grandmothers and aunts named Mary—all strong women. Today, for the same reason, we have four girls named Mary: MaryFrances (who goes by Francie), MaryMargaret (Maisie), MaryJane (Janie or JJ), and MaryTeresa (Tessa). (I am just Mary!) When we were deciding on a name for the ranch, Brian came up with Five Marys because we knew it would truly be a family affair, and it stuck.

Our four Heffernan girls may share part of a name—and a love of rodeo and pork chops with applesauce—but their personalities couldn't be more different. Each girl has her own strengths and doesn't hesitate to differentiate herself from her sisters.

Winter

On our ranch, winter is lambing season. Most people associate lambs with springtime, but our hardy Navajo-Churro sheep give birth in the winter, typically in December and January. Their heavy wool coats keep them warm (we even use old sheep's wool to keep our water troughs from freezing as easily at night), and the mommas are very good at keeping the lambs protected from the elements. When our sheep give birth to twins or triplets, some lambs wind up as "bottle babies" because they need extra human support. Our daughters nurse them back to health in our baby barn, feeding and warming them morning and night and generally making them part of the family. Sometimes our Great Pyrenees Beau even joins in, sleeping with the lambs he feels are particularly vulnerable.

It's a challenging time for us, though. We're still delivering hay to all the cows ourselves because the pastures don't usually turn green again before April. We calculated that Brian throws about 2 million pounds of feed to our cattle each year, from 1,500-pound bales. For the holidays, we always look forward to a brief respite and head to my parents' house in the Bay Area after a preholiday meat-shipping frenzy. For Christmas, my dad is in charge of making a big prime rib while we enjoy my mom's annual holiday decorations. We celebrate Brian's and JJ's birthdays in February. In between, we hunker down as the valley gets blanketed in snow, taking advantage of the cold nights to make warming meals like lamb potpie, spicy meatballs, and pot roast. And there's always a lot of baking, especially by the girls, who spend more time indoors in the winter.

LITTLE HOUSE DINNER

Menu for 6 to 8

WHEN I WAS NINE, my parents decided to restore a historic home in what would someday become the booming Silicon Valley—in a place and time where most older houses were commonly scraped off and rebuilt from scratch. Over the years, one weekend project at a time, they turned a true diamond in the rough (we found the house up on blocks with 175 broken windowpanes and needing all-new electricity and plumbing!) into a gorgeous family home. But while they were doing the initial renovations, for over a year, my parents rented a tiny two-bedroom place and all four of us kids (including the baby, who we still call Baby Ann) shared a small bedroom. I have always remembered that time fondly. I loved sharing a room with my three siblings, staying up late and rearranging our beds together. I always wanted the same for my girls.

When we bought the ranch, we knew our girls would share a room in our 760-square-foot Little House at first, until we had the time and money to fix up the larger homestead (which we called the Big House) next door. The four of them shared a double bed at first, and then with the addition of an expanded attic space and a new staircase, they moved into one bigger lofted space in the Little House. Now, even with the spiffed-up Big House next door, we all still sleep together in the Little House. We're close enough to say good night to each other every night with our heads on our pillows. I love the sense of physical closeness our Little House provides.

The Little House's kitchen is an extension of that same ethos of small-space living. Our family does everything together, and sharing space is one of the things that teaches us how to be cooperative and flexible with each other. That's why even with my new, larger kitchen in the Big House, we still make dinner in the Little House sometimes. It's smaller, and there's no dishwasher, and we may bump into each other more as the girls grow—but nothing beats cooking together and sharing that small family table.

MENU TIPS

Because it's mostly made from pantry staples, this is a great dinner to have a few days to a week after you've been grocery shopping. Prep the kale and the bread while the pasta bakes, and while the pasta cools, roast the kale and the garlic bread together.

BRIAN IS FROM A FAMILY OF FOOD AND COCKTAIL LOVERS. When we hang out with all my in-laws, someone is always the evening's designated bartender. Since my signature cocktail is a sidecar, I'm a bourbon girl, but occasionally I love a cocktail with rye whiskey, which has a slightly spicier taste that I enjoy most in the winter. This take on a whiskey sour—made with rye instead of bourbon, and lightly sweetened with the syrup from my Homemade Cocktail Cherries (recipe follows) instead of simple syrup—has enough lemon that it reminds me of a sidecar but is a little less sweet. Make the cherries in the summer when you have fresh fruit on hand, or use frozen sour cherries in the winter. (If you'd like to use fresh or frozen sweet cherries, reduce the added sugar to ½ cup. You can also make the cherries without the booze, for kids or for stirring into yogurt.)

If you like a cocktail with a pretty layer of foam on top, add an egg white to the shaker.

RYE WHISKEY SOURS <u>WITH</u> HOMEMADE COCKTAIL CHERRIES

Makes 2 large or 4 smaller cocktails

Fill a large cocktail shaker with ice, then add the whiskey, syrup to taste, and lemon juice, and shake hard for a full 30 seconds. Fill 2 highball or 4 lowball glasses with ice, then strain the cocktail over the ice. Thread 2 cherries onto a cocktail skewer for each glass, then add an orange slice to the skewer, then a third cherry. Serve immediately.

1 cup American rye whiskey
4 to 5 tablespoons syrup from Homemade Cocktail Cherries, or 2 teaspoons superfine sugar
¼ cup freshly squeezed Meyer lemon (from 1 juicy large lemon or 2 smaller lemons) or regular lemon juice
6 to 12 Homemade Cocktail Cherries (recipe follows)
2 (¼-inch-thick) orange slices, halved

Homemade Cocktail Cherries

Makes about 3 cups

In a small saucepan, combine the cherries with the water, sugar, lemon zest, and salt. Bring to a boil over high heat, stirring until the sugar dissolves, then reduce to a simmer and cook for 5 minutes, stirring occasionally. Remove the pan from the heat and pick out and discard the lemon strip. Stir in the bourbon, then divide the cherries among three half-pint jars. Add the cooking liquid until it comes up to ½ inch below each jar's rim, then clean the rims, add the lids, and refrigerate until chilled. Serve in cocktails, or refrigerate for up to 2 weeks. You can also process the cherries according to the jar manufacturer's instructions for water-bath canning for 10 minutes, if desired, in which case they will be shelf stable for 6 months.

1 pound (about 3 cups) fresh or frozen sour cherries (pitted or not)
1 cup water
1 cup sugar
2-inch strip of lemon zest
Pinch of kosher salt
¼ cup bourbon, rye, or other whiskey (optional)

IN THIS EASIER TAKE ON SPAGHETTI AND MEATBALLS, everything from the dry-aged beef to the pasta gets cooked in one cast-iron pan, and you wind up with a family-friendly feast. The ingredient list might look long, but trust me, it comes together quickly. Make the meatballs as spicy as you want: using ¼ teaspoon of red pepper flakes adds a tinge of spice, but using 1 teaspoon makes them good and hot. You can roast the kale and the garlic bread together for efficiency's sake while the main event cools—it will stay hot for a long time.

ONE-PAN SPICY MEATBALL BAKE

Makes 6 to 8 servings

Preheat the oven to 400 degrees F.

In a large, deep ovenproof skillet (such as a 12-inch cast-iron skillet) or Dutch oven, heat 3 tablespoons of the olive oil over medium-high heat. Add the onion and cook, stirring, for 8 to 10 minutes, or until soft, browned, and beginning to stick to the pan. Season with ½ teaspoon salt and ¼ teaspoon black pepper.

Meanwhile, in a medium bowl, mash together the meat, oats, cheese, egg, garlic, oregano, red pepper flakes, 1 teaspoon salt, and ½ teaspoon black pepper until well blended. (You can use a fork, but I think hands work best.)

When the onions are ready, transfer them to a bowl and set aside. Add the remaining 2 tablespoons olive oil to the pan, then add the meat mixture by small handfuls. (They could also be meatball shaped, if you feel like taking the time to form them more properly.) Cook the meat for 8 to 10 minutes, turning occasionally once it releases easily from the pan but otherwise leaving it untouched, until the meat is browned all over. Scatter the onions over the meat, then add the pasta, sauce, tomatoes, and boiling water. Stir gently to release the meat from the pan, breaking it up slightly and incorporating the water into the mixture. (It's OK if the meat breaks up a bit; you want some of it on the top.) Press down any pasta that hasn't gotten wet.

Carefully cover and seal the pan with aluminum foil or a lid (if you have one) and bake on the middle rack for 20 minutes. Uncover the pan, give everything a good stir, and then bake for another 15 to 20 minutes uncovered, or until the pasta is cooked through and beginning to crisp on the top and most of the liquid has been absorbed. Let the pan sit for 10 minutes, then shower with extra cheese and the basil and serve piping hot.

5 tablespoons extra-virgin olive oil, divided
1 medium yellow onion, halved and thinly sliced
Kosher salt and freshly ground black pepper
1 pound ground beef, lamb, or pork
½ cup quick-cooking oats
½ cup (about 2 ounces) ground Parmesan cheese, plus more for serving
1 large egg
3 cloves garlic, minced
1 teaspoon dried oregano
¼ to 1 teaspoon red pepper flakes (optional)
1 pound rigatoni, fusilli, or other short dried pasta
1 (25-ounce) jar of your favorite tomato-based pasta sauce
2 roma or beefsteak tomatoes (about ¾ pound), chopped
4 cups boiling water
Torn leaves from 2 or 3 large sprigs fresh basil, for serving

IF YOU'VE NEVER TRIED KALE CHIPS or crispy kale, you're in for a treat. Start with the healthiest-looking green in the produce section, swipe it with flavorful oil, dust it with salt and spices, roast it until crisp, and you've got a crunchy snack or side dish as alluring as potato chips—but a whole lot more nutritious. We love making it with the M5 Spice Rub we sell on our website, but you can make it at home too. In a small bowl, mix together 1½ teaspoons kosher salt, 1 teaspoon red pepper flakes, ½ teaspoon each of dried rosemary, dried thyme, and flaky sea salt, and a pinch each of freshly ground black pepper and garlic powder. You'll end up with about 1½ tablespoons, which can be scaled up as needed. Use a teaspoon of the rub here, and save the rest for seasoning steaks, burgers, or Sweet Potato Waffle Fries (page 203).

If you double the kale recipe, use two pans, reduce the oven temperature to 350 degrees F, and cook the kale longer (more like 20 to 25 minutes), rotating the pans halfway through. The increased amount of kale amps up the moisture in the oven, so it will take longer to dry and crisp.

M5-RUBBED CRISPY KALE

Makes 6 to 8 servings

Preheat the oven to 400 degrees F.

Pile the kale on a large baking sheet. Drizzle with the olive oil, then mix and rub and toss the kale and oil together until every piece of kale is coated lightly with oil. Sprinkle the spice rub carefully and evenly over the greens (otherwise you'll get all the salt in one bite), then toss and mix again. Spread the kale evenly across the pan.

Roast on the middle or bottom rack for 10 minutes. (It's fine to put the kale in the oven with something else, like the Anytime Sourdough Garlic Bread on page 22.) Stir the kale and cook for another 5 to 7 minutes, until the kale is crisp and browned in spots. Transfer to a serving bowl and serve warm or at room temperature.

8 ounces torn kale (about 8 packed cups), from 2 (8-ounce) bunches kale (any color or type), center ribs removed and leaves torn into roughly 2-inch pieces

3 tablespoons extra-virgin olive oil

1 scant teaspoon M5 Spice Rub (see headnote)

I LOVE RURAL LIFE, but it's still hard for me to be twenty minutes away from a decent-size grocery store. When I shop, I try to think through my week carefully, piling my cart with not only what I know I'll need, but also what I know I'll want in case, say, snow closes the mountain pass that separates me from that grocery store. I always buy fresh produce, but I'm careful to also stock up on pantry and freezer staples—things like beans, grains, pasta, spices, cheeses, breads, and baking ingredients. I often buy sourdough baguettes and freeze them in case we want to make this garlic bread my girls love. Smeared with a mixture of butter, olive oil, Parmesan, and herbs, it's simple to make and always a crowd favorite.

ANYTIME SOURDOUGH GARLIC BREAD

Makes 6 to 8 servings

Preheat the oven to 400 degrees F. Line a baking sheet with parchment paper.

Cut the baguette in half crosswise, then cut each half in half again lengthwise, so you have four forearm-length baguette sections. Arrange them on the baking sheet cut sides up.

In a small mixing bowl, use a fork to mash together the butter, cheese, olive oil, garlic powder, herbs, salt, and pepper until blended. Smear the butter mixture on the baguette pieces. (You can prepare the bread up to this point and freeze it with the buttered sides together, then thaw it on the counter for a few hours before baking.) Bake for 12 to 15 minutes, or until the edges of the bread have browned nicely. Cut each section into thirds or quarters and serve warm.

1-pound sourdough baguette (roughly 20 inches long)
10 tablespoons (1¼ sticks) unsalted butter, softened
½ cup ground Parmesan or Pecorino cheese
¼ cup extra-virgin olive oil
2 teaspoons garlic powder
1½ teaspoons dried herbs (such as thyme, rosemary, oregano, or a mix of the three)
1 teaspoon kosher salt
1 teaspoon freshly ground black pepper

I GREW UP BAKING COOKIES with my mom, but they were usually one *type* of cookie, like chocolate chip, or peanut butter, or molasses. But cookies stuffed with a whole rainbow of ingredients—call them everything cookies, leftover cookies, or kitchen-sink cookies—are relatively new to the cookie scene. My girls know how great it is to bite into a chocolate chip cookie laced with the perfect mix of sweet and salty add-ins. The problem? No one's perfect kitchen-sink cookie is perfect for everyone. That's why I based my recipe on adding various categories of ingredients, instead of specific ones—so you can add pretzels, potato chips, or popcorn for your "salty, crunchy stuff," and choose whatever chocolaty, nutty, and chewy stuff you want to create your own ideal combination.

If you're the type of person who needs exact measurements, see below, but you can also pretty much chuck in whatever you want as long as the ingredients are the size of a thumbnail or smaller, and you have about 5 cups total of add-ins.

These cookies are ideal for giant ice cream sandwiches, and they also make great cookie bars (see Note)—in which case, they totally qualify as breakfast bars in my book.

RANCH-SIZE KITCHEN-SINK COOKIES

Makes 12 large cookies

Preheat the oven to 350 degrees F. Line a baking sheet with parchment paper and set aside.

In a medium mixing bowl, whisk together the flour, baking powder, baking soda, and salt and set aside.

In the bowl of a stand mixer fitted with the paddle attachment (or using an electric hand mixer), beat the butter and brown sugar together on medium speed for 1 minute, until a shade lighter in color. Add the eggs one at a time, mixing on medium speed and scraping down the sides and bottom of the bowl between additions, then add the vanilla and mix for 30 seconds on medium speed.

Scrape down the bowl again, then add the flour mixture. Pulse the machine on and off to start incorporating the flour, then mix on low speed until no white spots remain in the dough, about 15 seconds.

Add the chocolate, nuts, salty stuff, and sweet stuff, and mix on low speed for another few seconds to break up any large clumps. Remove the paddle and use a wooden spoon to turn and mix the batter, making sure the ingredients are well distributed.

➡

2 cups all-purpose flour
1 teaspoon baking powder
½ teaspoon baking soda
½ teaspoon kosher salt
1 cup (2 sticks) unsalted butter, at room temperature
1 packed cup light brown sugar
2 large eggs
2 teaspoons vanilla extract
1½ cups chocolaty stuff (such as chunks, chips, or chopped chocolate of any type)
1½ cups nutty stuff (such as walnuts, pecans, almonds, peanuts, pistachios, or hazelnuts)
1 cup salty, crunchy stuff (such as pretzels, filled pretzels, potato chips, or popcorn)
1 cup sweet, chewy stuff (such as dried cherries, dried cranberries, raisins, chopped dates, small candies, cereal, or shredded coconut)
Flaky sea salt

Form 6 big mounds of dough, each a scant ½ cup, and stagger them on the prepared baking sheet. Press them into 1-inch-thick discs and sprinkle with the sea salt. Refrigerate the remaining dough. (You can also form the discs and refrigerate, covered, until ready to bake, up to 3 days. Increase the baking time by 4 minutes if baking from cold.)

Bake the cookies for 17 to 20 minutes, or until just beginning to brown at the edges and crack in the centers. Cool for 5 minutes on the sheet, then transfer the cookies to a wire rack to cool completely. Repeat with the remaining dough. (You can bake all the cookies on two sheets at the same time, rotating the sheets halfway through baking, but they'll wind up slightly different sizes.)

Store the cooled cookies in an airtight container at room temperature for up to 5 days.

NOTE: To make these as cookie bars, press the batter into a greased 9-by-13-inch baking pan, then bake at 350 degrees F for 25 minutes, or until brown on the edges and firm in the center. Cool for 30 minutes, then transfer the bars to a large cutting board and cut into 24 rectangles. Cool completely before serving or storing.

DIY: WOOL POM-POM GARLANDS

MY MOM IS A BORN DECORATOR. During the holidays, there are wintry scenes made with lead figurines on the windowsills in her house, gorgeous wreaths on doors and walls, and a trail of garlands up the stairs. She's the kind of person who repaints her front door almost yearly, just for fun—and I follow right in her footsteps. I love making our Little House look special for any occasion, from birthdays to Halloween to the Fourth of July. Adorable pom-pom garlands, made with felted wool, are an easy-to-make accent I use when I want to spiff up the house between celebrations, just because.

Hang them in front of a window or mirror, use them to decorate a holiday tree, or drape them from a mantle. If you make large ones but don't roll them very long after rinsing them, they make great faux snowballs. Creating the pom-poms will take about half a day to complete.

Makes about 6 dozen large or 12 dozen small pom-poms, enough for 3 (roughly 6-foot) garlands

First, using your fingertips and starting with the loose end of one of the balls of wool roving, pull off a piece of roving with your fingertips—it should come off the ball like cotton candy, leaving you with a little tuft of wool fluff. Repeat 20 more times or so, until you have a pile of fluff about the size of a large sandwich. Repeat with the rest of the first ball of roving until you have about 24 piles. (They should each weigh about 10 grams, or ⅓ ounce, but you don't need to get that technical, as long as all of the piles are roughly equal for similar-size pom-poms. A 10-gram pile will result in pom-poms about the size of golf balls, but you could also make smaller pom-poms with 5-gram piles.)

In a large mixing bowl, whisk together 1 tablespoon of the dish soap with about 1 cup of hot tap water until sudsy. Add another 7 cups of hot water.

Working with 1 pile of wool on a clean counter, separate the fibers into a space about as big as a sheet of paper, peeling apart any heftier hunks of wool as you go. Wet your hands in the soapy water. Starting from one corner, roll the wool into a ball, folding inward from the sides (like folding over the sides of a burrito) and filling in any indentations as you go, until you have a neat little rolled bundle of wool.

3 (8-ounce) skeins natural wool roving, in assorted colors
2 tablespoons dish soap, divided
Hot tap water
Rubber dishwashing gloves, as needed
Needle and thread or embroidery floss
Thimble, as needed

➤——➤

Working next to a sink, submerge the bundle in the hot, soapy water, take it out, and use your hands to roll the ball into a smaller, tighter ball—you'll feel it collapse into a heap first, but as you work it, squeezing and rolling between your palms, it will begin to get smaller and take on a ball shape. (I find it easiest to roll the ball with one cupped hand, using my other flat palm as a rolling surface. Some people like wearing rubber dishwashing gloves for this process, so try both and see what works best for you.) Dip the ball into the soapy water again and repeat, until you have a very soapy ball of wool. Next, run the ball under hot tap water, squeezing and rinsing and rolling until it feels clean and looks more or less like a hairy golf ball, rearranging the wool as necessary as you go to create as round a shape as possible. (You can trim away any stubborn stray strands of wool with scissors, or if your ball seems a little lopsided, wind a few fresh strands of wool fiber around the ball to help tuck in any lumps.) Keep rolling to rid the ball of any excess water, applying more pressure as the ball becomes tighter. When the ball starts to feel compact and the surface looks uniform, after 2 to 4 minutes of constant rolling, the pom-pom is done. Set aside to dry on a kitchen towel.

Repeat with the remaining wool piles, replacing the soapy water with a new hot batch about halfway through, once the water starts to cool down. Repeat the entire process with the remaining 2 skeins of roving. Dry the pom-poms for 1 to 2 days, turning occasionally.

Using a needle and the help of a thimble, if necessary, string the pom-poms onto thread or embroidery floss with the desired spacing between each ball. (You can tie knots on either side of each ball if you wish, but if your pom-poms are tight enough, they shouldn't slide along the thread very easily.) Time to decorate!

SNOW DAY DINNER

Menu for 6

IT MAY COME AS A SURPRISE that our California ranch gets snow. But it's a big state, and we're at the very northern tip of it—and at altitude, so we get all kinds of weather in the winter and spring. Waking up to a glittering white blanket is still a huge thrill for the girls, but it also means more work around the ranch. We have to make sure the animals have dry bedding and extra feed, so when the snow is too deep for the trucks, we get up earlier than usual to haul hay and feed up into the hills with the tractor. We always appreciate how well suited our animals are to our environment, even when it snows. Our Navajo-Churro sheep have such insulating wool that snow piles up on their backs without melting. The pigs keep each other warm in the barn, and the cattle's coats grow thicker in the winter.

Once our morning chores are finished, it becomes a more typical snow day: the girls warm up by the fire and play board games until they're thawed enough to go outside again to play, and I usually turn my attention to a cooking project with who-ever's had enough with the snowmen. (If we're making anything with chocolate, that would be Francie.) In the afternoon, we gear up to do the chores again before nightfall, adding bedding and feed so the animals are warm and dry and well fed throughout the night.

Then it's our turn to eat. Snow days invariably mean hearty comfort food, like a lamb potpie topped with a gigantic flaky biscuit, served with a salad of bitter greens, bacon ends, and croutons toasted in bacon fat. It's a meal that warms us, inside and out.

MENU TIPS

If you want to render the lard the same day you bake the potpie, you'll need to do it first thing in the morning so the lard has time to cool before you use it in the crust. The salad comes together in about the same amount of time it takes for the potpie to bake.

FROM CLASSIC SHEPHERD'S PIE TO HANDHELD BEEF PASTIES (page 217), everyone in our family loves the combination of flavorful meat, chunky vegetables, and flaky crust. On cold, wintry days, I make this version with lamb, carrots, parsnips, and potatoes simmered in a red wine–tomato broth with thyme and smoky Spanish paprika. I top it with what's really a giant homemade biscuit, made with lard from our own pigs. (For more on rendering leaf lard for pie crust or biscuits, see page 39.) Using ground lamb instead of stew meat means it doesn't need to simmer for hours, so the whole thing comes together in about ninety minutes.

You'll need a 12-inch or similar cast-iron pan for this dish.

LAMB AND ROOT VEGETABLE POTPIE WITH LEAF LARD BISCUIT CRUST

Makes 6 servings

Preheat the oven to 400 degrees F and position a rack in the center of the oven.

First, make the filling. Heat a 12-inch cast-iron skillet over medium-high heat. Add the lamb, season with salt and pepper, and cook, stirring occasionally to break up the meat, until cooked through and browned in spots, about 5 minutes. Using a slotted spoon, transfer the lamb to a bowl, leaving the fat in the pan. (You should have about 2 tablespoons; if you don't think there's quite enough, add a swirl of olive oil.) Reduce the heat to medium, add the onion, and season with salt and pepper, then cook, stirring frequently, until softened, about 3 minutes. Add the potatoes, carrots, and parsnips, season again, and cook for another 10 minutes, or until the vegetables are browned in spots and beginning to soften. Add the garlic and thyme and stir for 1 minute, then add the tomato paste and paprika, stirring until totally incorporated. Add the red wine and cook for 1 minute, stirring and scraping any browned bits from the bottom of the pan. Add the broth and bring to a boil, then stir in the lamb and reduce the heat to maintain a simmer. In a small bowl, whisk together the cold water and cornstarch until smooth, then carefully stir the mixture into the filling. (The pan will be quite full.) Cook for 10 minutes, stirring occasionally, or until the vegetables are just tender. Stir in the Dijon, season to taste with salt and pepper, and remove the pan from the heat.

■——→

ingredients continue

FOR THE FILLING
1 pound ground lamb
Kosher salt and freshly ground black pepper
Olive oil, as needed
1 medium yellow onion, chopped
1½ pounds Yukon Gold potatoes (about 4 medium), cut into ½-inch pieces
1 pound carrots (about 5 large), cut into ½-inch pieces
1 pound parsnips (about 4 large), cut into ½-inch pieces
5 large cloves garlic, minced
2 tablespoons chopped fresh thyme, or 2 teaspoons dried thyme
1 tablespoon tomato paste
½ teaspoon smoked Spanish paprika or regular paprika
½ cup dry red wine
3 cups beef bone broth
¼ cup cold water
2 tablespoons cornstarch
2 tablespoons Dijon mustard

While the filling simmers, make the crust. In a large mixing bowl, whisk together the flour, baking powder, and kosher salt. Add the lard and, using your fingers, a pastry cutter, or two knives, work the lard into the flour mixture until it's evenly sandy and a little ragged looking—all the fat should be broken into pea-size pieces or smaller. Add 1 cup of the cream and, using a fork, stir the mixture until most of the cream has been absorbed. Use your hands to gently knead the dough a few times in the bowl, gathering up any dry spots as you go and adding the last 1 or 2 tablespoons of cream if necessary to make the last bit of flour in the bottom of the bowl stick together. Transfer the dough to a well-floured board and pat into an 8-inch round. (It's OK if it's crumbly.) Fold the dough in half, then in half again (this will create good layers in the crust), then use a rolling pin to roll it into a rough 12-inch round, adding flour to avoid sticking as needed. Brush away any extra flour. Brush the entire round with the beaten egg, then sprinkle with sea salt.

Carefully transfer the dough to cover the filling. (You can use your hands and forearms to move the dough, or use the board to slide it onto the filling.) Gently fold the edges of the dough under where they overlap the edges of the pan, then use a small, sharp knife to cut six 3-inch-long slits through the dough in a starburst pattern. These will let steam escape as the potpie bakes.

Place the skillet on a baking sheet and bake for 25 minutes, or until the crust is a deep golden brown. Let the potpie rest for 10 minutes, then serve hot.

NOTE: To make ahead, prepare the filling as instructed, cool to room temperature, and refrigerate for up to 3 days. Prepare the dough and transfer the round to a baking sheet, cover, and refrigerate for up to 24 hours. Before baking, first reheat the filling in the skillet at 400 degrees F for 15 to 20 minutes, until bubbling around the edges, then stir; carefully top with the pastry and bake as directed.

FOR THE CRUST

2½ cups all-purpose flour, plus more for forming the dough

1 tablespoon baking powder

1 teaspoon kosher salt

8 tablespoons (4 ounces) cold rendered leaf lard (see page 39), regular lard, or unsalted butter, cut into 8 pieces

1 cup plus 1 to 2 tablespoons cold heavy cream, divided

1 large egg, beaten

Flaky sea salt

LEAF LARD BISCUITS

You can make delicious, fluffy biscuits with the same dough you use to top the potpie. Prepare only the crust ingredients as directed, stopping once you've formed an 8-inch round. Using a floured 3-inch biscuit cutter or similar, cut out 6 biscuits and carefully transfer them to a parchment-lined baking sheet or snuggle them in a pie pan. (You can gather and pat the scraps into an even layer and cut out 2 additional biscuits, if desired.) Brush the tops of the biscuits with the beaten egg and sprinkle with sea salt. Bake at 400 degrees F for 18 to 20 minutes, or until puffed and golden brown. Cool for 5 minutes before serving. *(Makes 6 to 8 biscuits.)*

DIY: SLOW-COOKER PIE LARD

LEAF LARD IS THE FAT from the area around a hog's kidneys—so named because when it comes out of the animal, it has a roughly leaf-like shape. When it's rendered, or melted, it creates a smooth, almost flavorless fat that makes for the flakiest biscuits and pie crusts. (Unlike butter, rendered leaf lard doesn't contain any water, which can make crusts tough if the butter melts before the dough goes into the oven.) Some people swear it's the only way to make perfectly tender pastry. While making it means an extra step compared to store-bought, I really love being able to use as many parts of the pig as possible. It's well suited for a savory crust (see page 35), but it's also great for sweet pies—use it as a substitute for the butter in my All-Purpose Double Pie Crust (page 166).

Freezing the leaf lard for about 30 minutes before you begin makes it much easier to cut.

Makes about 2 cups (depending on lard size)

Using a sharp knife, cut the lard into ¼-inch cubes, trimming and discarding any pinkish meat or discolored bits that may still be attached. (These will add porky flavor and color to your final product, which should taste very neutral and be completely snow white once it has solidified.) Transfer the lard to a slow cooker and cook on low for 6 hours, stirring once or twice, or until about three-quarters of the lard has liquefied. (Some solid pieces might refuse to melt.)

Line a fine-mesh sieve with four layers of cheesecloth, and set the sieve over a large bowl. Scoop a few ladlefuls of fat and bits into the cheesecloth, allowing it to drain fully before adding more. When all the fat has drained into the bowl, use a wooden spoon to press gently on the solid bits to release as much liquid as possible, then wrap the cheesecloth around the bits and squeeze out any remaining fat. Discard the cheesecloth and solids.

Transfer the liquid to a mason jar and let cool to room temperature with the lid off (it will solidify and turn from yellowish clear to snow-white lard), then seal and refrigerate for up to 2 weeks or freeze for up to 3 months.

1 piece leaf lard (1¼ to 2 pounds), frozen for 30 minutes
Large (6 quart) slow cooker
Fine-mesh sieve
Cheesecloth

GROWING UP, I WAS THE KID WHO *LOVED* GREENS. My mom made the best fresh salads most nights for dinner and served them with a simple dressing—just good-quality olive oil and an heirloom vinegar that we made at home with a starter that has been in my family for generations. (It packs a punch!) I was always the salad dresser and I liked my dressings extra sharp.

Today, I don't always have the homemade vinegar on hand, but I still make vinaigrettes with a good, strong bite. Here's a great example: a salad of sturdy mixed lettuces dressed with a warm bacon vinaigrette that pairs perfectly with a rich meal, like the potpie on page 35.

WINTER SALAD WITH BACON-END VINAIGRETTE AND RANCH-SIZE CROUTONS

Makes 6 to 8 servings as a side or 4 servings as a meal

In a large skillet, heat 1 tablespoon of the olive oil over medium-low heat. Add the bacon ends, and cook, stirring frequently, until the bacon has given off its fat and begins to crisp, about 5 minutes. Using a slotted spoon, transfer the bacon to a plate, leaving the fat behind. Add the bread cubes, tossing and stirring to coat them all in a little fat, then season liberally with salt and pepper and cook, turning frequently, until the cubes are toasted on all sides, about 4 minutes total. Transfer the croutons to a large salad bowl.

Return the bacon to the pan over medium heat. Add 2 tablespoons of the olive oil. Add the shallots and cook, stirring, until they begin to crisp, about 3 minutes. Remove the pan from the heat and stir in the champagne vinegar and the remaining 2 tablespoons olive oil. Season with salt and pepper. (If you want to make the salad ahead a bit, you can set what you've done aside up for up to 1 hour and rewarm the vinaigrette over very low heat for a few minutes just before serving.)

Add the radicchio, romaine, and red leaf lettuce to the salad bowl. Scrape in the vinaigrette and bacon, toss to coat all the leaves evenly with the vinaigrette, and serve immediately.

5 tablespoons extra-virgin olive oil, divided
½ pound bacon ends or roughly chopped bacon, cut into 1-inch pieces if large
4 cups 1-inch bread cubes (from about 8 ounces hearty bread)
Kosher salt and freshly ground black pepper
1 large shallot, finely chopped, or 2 tablespoons finely chopped red onion
¼ cup champagne vinegar
2 cups chopped radicchio (from half a 6-ounce head) or endive (from 2 medium heads)
2 cups chopped romaine lettuce (about 3 ounces)
4 cups chopped red leaf lettuce (from 1 small head)

FRANCIE IS BECOMING AN EXCELLENT BAKER and is our house chocolate fanatic—she'll proudly tell you that one of her favorite breakfasts-in-a-hurry is eating Nutella from the jar. For her, I've developed a triple-chocolate brownie, made with her signature morning snack, dark cocoa powder, and semisweet chocolate. Make these a little chewier by baking them in a larger pan, or more gooey in the center by using a smaller one. Either way, you'll get a deep, nutty flavor from the combination of chocolate-hazelnut spread and browned butter, as well as a perfect brownie's signature crackly, shiny top.

FRANCIE'S BROWNIES

Makes 16 brownies

Preheat the oven to 350 degrees F. Grease an 8-inch square baking pan (for gooey brownies) or a 9-by-13-inch baking pan (for chewier brownies) with butter, even if the pan is nonstick, and set aside.

In a small saucepan, melt the butter over medium heat. Continue cooking, swirling the pan occasionally, until the milk solids in the butter are medium brown and the butter takes on a sweet, nutty smell, 5 to 7 minutes. Remove the pan from the heat, wait a few moments for any popping and bubbling to stop, add the chocolate chips, and whisk until all the chocolate has melted.

Meanwhile, in the bowl of a stand mixer fitted with the paddle attachment (or using an electric hand mixer), beat the eggs and both sugars on medium-high speed for about 4 minutes, until very light, stopping to scrape down the bowl after the first minute. With the mixer on low, add the melted chocolate and mix to combine. Add the cocoa and sea salt and mix on low until all the cocoa is incorporated, then add the sour cream and mix just to blend. Add the flour and mix on low until fully incorporated, scraping the sides of the bowl as needed, then add the chocolate-hazelnut spread, increase the speed to medium, and beat for 2 minutes.

Scrape the batter into the prepared pan and spread into an even layer. Bake for about 30 minutes for a 9-by-13-inch pan or 50 to 55 minutes for an 8-inch pan, or until puffed and cracked and a tooth-pick inserted into the brownies halfway between the center and one edge of the pan comes out with a few moist crumbs attached. Cool in the pan at least 1 hour if you want to eat them warm, or cool completely for easy cutting and serve at room temperature.

Cover and store the brownies at room temperature for up to 3 days.

½ cup (1 stick) unsalted butter, cut into cubes, plus more for greasing the pan
1 cup semisweet chocolate chips
5 large eggs
¾ cup packed dark brown sugar
½ cup granulated sugar
½ cup Dutch-process cocoa powder
½ teaspoon fine sea salt
½ cup sour cream
1 cup all-purpose flour
1 cup chocolate-hazelnut spread (such as Nutella)

WINTER ON THE RANCH means we leave the house in the mornings with extra tools. Since the animals' water troughs often freeze overnight in low temps, Brian and I—and sometimes the girls—often bundle up and set out with axes and shovels to break up the solid ice blocks that form on the top of each trough. We feed the cattle on the hill from the feed truck, and the snow makes for a beautiful sight, but it can be tough to navigate the frozen ground.

At the end of a long snowy day, I want nothing more than to curl up in front of our woodstove with a hot toddy and watch the icicles forming on the roof drip in the glow of the house lights. I make my toddies using a honey-based simple syrup, the juice of a whole lemon, a pinch of cayenne for extra heat, and our Five Marys bourbon.

MEYER LEMON HOT TODDIES WITH A KICK

Makes 2 toddies

In a small saucepan, combine the water and honey to taste and bring to a boil over high heat. Add the bourbon, lemon juice, and cayenne to taste. Whisk to distribute the cayenne evenly. Transfer to two 12-ounce mugs, top each with a lemon slice, and enjoy immediately.

1½ cups water
⅓ to ½ cup good-quality honey
¼ cup bourbon, such as Five Marys Nothin's Easy Bourbon
¼ cup freshly squeezed Meyer lemon or regular lemon juice (from 1 juicy large lemon or 2 smaller lemons)
Pinch of cayenne
2 thin lemon slices

MAKE-AHEAD DINNER FOR SIX

Menu for 6

WE START LAMBING IN JANUARY on the ranch. It's the best time for our hearty winter breed of Navajo-Churro sheep to give birth because the babies are ready to start grazing just as the spring grasses are popping up. When lambing season comes on, we suddenly have over two hundred newborn lambs *baaa*ing about in search of the right momma. And because we have coyotes, bears, and mountain lions on our property, every last lamb has to be accounted for and closed into the barn every night for safety.

Taking care of the lambs falls mostly to the girls. They are great at herding the lambs and ewes in—and way more patient than I am. They usually start the process in our ATVs, riding along the perimeters to check for any of them sleeping along the fence line. The mommas know that this signal means it's time to head for the barns to bed down for the night, but the process of slowly walking them all in as the light fades, with baby lambs that sometimes aren't even a day old, takes time. (Maisie and Francie once built a sled to transport the littlest ones in more easily.) When lambing season is in full swing, there's often a lamb that's been rejected by its mother—common when ewes have twins or triplets—and the girls have to set it up as a "bottle baby" and feed it in the small barn by the house. Once the sheep are all safe inside, the girls usually have a bottle baby or two to feed. Then they move on to their other responsibilities, like feeding their horses and 4-H steers and doing whatever homework they didn't finish.

Because of this, lambing season is when my make-ahead meals help make dinners more manageable. The more I can do between a morning shipping out meat and the afternoon lamb-wrangling sessions, in less time, the better. My pot roast—something you can throw into the slow cooker and walk away from, then remember when everyone comes inside at once hungry and *ready* for dinner—is a lifesaver. If you have time to make rolls ahead of time, you can prepare the dough and store it in the fridge, and see if you can get the kids to make a super-simple dessert with California's best winter citrus. Otherwise, just steam some vegetables and open the slow cooker for an all-in-one meal you'll come back to again and again.

MENU TIPS

You can prep both the pot roast and the rolls in the morning and they'll be ready to bake at dinnertime—just pop them into the oven before you set the table and slice the roast.

THIS SLOW-COOKER STAPLE IS one of our go-tos for several reasons. First, it requires zero babysitting, so it's perfect for even our busiest day on the ranch. Second, it's two dishes in one: the braised roast comes out meltingly tender, and the sweet potatoes, which hold their shape nicely as they cook, are perfectly mashable, already seasoned, and ready to serve. Third, because it relies mostly on pantry staples and comes together quickly, it's a great way to introduce kids to cooking family meals. And the soda is a cool trick: it tenderizes the meat and sweetens it ever so slightly, without adding any actual cola flavor.

You can also make this a day or two ahead and reheat—or even use a multicooker (see Note).

WALK-AWAY POT ROAST <u>WITH</u> MASHED SWEET POTATOES

Makes 6 servings

In a slow cooker, whisk together the broth, tomato sauce, cola, ginger, salt, onion powder, thyme, pepper, garlic powder, and bay leaf. Season the roast all over with salt and pepper and place it in the liquid. Nestle the potatoes around the roast (it's OK if they're not all submerged) and cook on low heat for 10 hours. (If you'd really like to work ahead, you can cook the roast, let it cool to room temperature, and refrigerate for up to 3 days. Before serving, remove the layer of fat that has formed on top, return to the slow cooker on high heat for 1 hour, then proceed as directed.)

Transfer the roast to a cutting board and remove any strings. Transfer the sweet potatoes to a serving bowl, use a fork to mash them, season to taste with salt and pepper, and cover with a plate to keep warm. Use a large shallow spoon or a turkey baster to skim as much fat as desired off the top of the liquid in the slow cooker. Slice the meat into 1-inch-thick slabs or cut it into 6 large hunks, transfer to a large shallow serving bowl, and drizzle with about 1 cup of the cooking juices. Serve immediately.

NOTE: To make this in a multicooker, cut the roast in half lengthwise before you put it into the pot, and make sure all the ingredients are well below the cooker's "max" line. You may not be able to fit all the sweet potatoes, so just cut 2 of them to start. Cook for 40 minutes on the "meat/stew" setting, then allow the pressure to release naturally for 20 minutes. Proceed as directed.

2 cups beef bone broth

1 (15-ounce) can tomato sauce

1 (12-ounce) can regular cola

1 (2-inch) piece ginger, peeled and cut into ¼-inch-thick coins

2 teaspoons kosher salt

1½ teaspoons onion powder

1 teaspoon dried thyme

½ teaspoon freshly ground black pepper

½ teaspoon garlic powder

1 dried bay leaf

1 (4-pound) boneless beef cross rib roast or chuck roast (any strings left intact)

3 large sweet potatoes (about 2½ pounds), cut into 2-inch chunks

WE LOVE HAVING ROLLS WITH DINNER—and I usually double any recipe so we have enough for the next day's breakfast—but sometimes getting organized enough to time my baking and have piping-hot rolls right when dinner hits the table is difficult. Enter my icebox rolls, which are super convenient because they can rise in the fridge.

While the sweet, yeasty dough will rise beautifully at room temperature, the refrigerator actually slows down the rising process, which means you can make it in the morning when you have time and have a much larger window for baking the rolls whenever you're ready. The optimal refrigerator-rising time is between 8 and 10 hours, but the dough can be refrigerated anywhere from 6 to 12 hours.

ICEBOX PULL-APART ROLLS

Makes 12 rolls

In the bowl of a stand mixer fitted with the dough hook (or in a large mixing bowl), whisk together the warm water and yeast and set aside for about 5 minutes, or until the mixture becomes foamy.

Meanwhile, generously grease a 9-by-13-inch pan with butter and set aside.

Add 2 cups of the flour and the milk to the mixer bowl, and stir on low speed (or by hand with a wooden spoon) until blended, about 1 minute. Add another cup of flour, plus 2 tablespoons of the melted butter, the honey, and salt, and mix on low speed until thoroughly mixed. Continue mixing on low speed until the dough becomes elastic and cleans the sides of the bowl, adding more flour 1 table-spoon at a time as needed. (If you're working by hand, switch from stirring to hand-kneading when the dough becomes too difficult to stir.) Increase the speed to medium and knead for 5 minutes (or 6 minutes by hand). The dough will be sticky.

Rub your hands with about 1 teaspoon of softened butter, then transfer the dough to a clean board, rubbing your hands over the dough and the board as you go. (This will prevent sticking.) Form the dough into a roughly 6-inch square, then cut into 12 pieces of roughly equal size. Working with one piece of dough at a time, form it into a ball, folding the outer edges underneath on all sides and pinching the dough together on the bottom, so it looks smooth and roundish on top. Repeat with each piece, rubbing your palms with a bit of room-temperature butter before forming the next ball, so each piece of dough is a bit shiny. Arrange the balls smooth sides

1 cup warm tap water (about 110 degrees F)
1 tablespoon active dry yeast
3 tablespoons unsalted butter, melted, divided, plus more at room temperature for greasing the pan and forming the rolls
3 to 3½ cups all-purpose flour, divided
½ cup whole milk
1½ tablespoons honey
½ teaspoon kosher salt
Vegetable oil spray

■—→

up in the prepared pan, spacing them evenly. Cover the pan with plastic wrap sprayed lightly with vegetable oil (the plastic should prevent air flow but shouldn't touch the rolls) and refrigerate for 8 to 10 hours, or until the rolls have about doubled in size and almost obscure the bottom of the pan. (Alternatively, you can let the rolls rise at room temperature, loosely covered, for 1 hour, or until doubled in size.)

When ready to bake, preheat the oven to 400 degrees F. Set out the pan at room temperature and remove the plastic. When the oven is hot, bake the rolls on the middle rack for 15 to 18 minutes, or until puffed and golden. Brush with the remaining tablespoon of melted butter. Let cool for 5 minutes, then break apart and serve hot, or transfer to a rack to cool completely. Store any uneaten rolls at room temperature, wrapped in plastic, for up to 3 days.

STEAMED BROCCOLI WITH MAYO

One of our family's favorite vegetable side dishes couldn't be simpler, but it often surprises people: we love to dip steamed broccoli in mayonnaise. In my house growing up, there was always a bowl of mayonnaise on the table when we had vegetables. My mom would make her "secret sauce" as a way of getting us excited about eating broccoli or green beans or asparagus. (Her big secret? Adding a little ketchup.) Today, I often spike the mayonnaise with chili-garlic sauce, soy sauce, or even our M5 Spice Rub (see page 21). Dare you to try it: just briefly steam broccoli (think 2 or 3 minutes) so it's still a bit crunchy, then serve it with a side of mayo, doctored however you want!

SOMETIMES DESSERT DOESN'T NEED TO BE A HUGE PRODUCTION. Take this simple dish: gorgeous California citrus is piled onto vanilla ice cream, drizzled with quality extra-virgin olive oil, and sprinkled with sea salt. There's no baking involved and you can prepare most of it ahead, but it blindsides you with flavor. I make it in the winter, even though it's not hot outside, because that's when California citrus is at its best.

CALIFORNIA CITRUS WITH VANILLA ICE CREAM AND SEA SALT

Makes 6 servings

You will need to cut the "supremes," or individual sections, out of the pithy structure of each citrus fruit: First, working with a small sharp knife, cut the stem and blossom ends off the fruit, then arrange it on a cutting board with one flat side down. Next, use the knife to cut off the peel and all white pith underneath in ½-inch strips, cutting in an arc around the flesh from the top of the fruit down to the cutting board. You will be left with a glistening orb with white vertical stripes running through it where the segments are still intact. Finally, cut on either side of each white stripe to cut out the individual segments. (It's tricky at first, but after a few slices you'll get the hang of it.) Pick out and discard any seeds you encounter along the way. You can supreme all of the citrus up to a day ahead and refrigerate the supremes, covered, until ready to serve.

To serve, scoop vanilla ice cream into six bowls, pile on the citrus, drizzle with olive oil, and sprinkle with sea salt.

6 citrus fruits (such as Valencia, Cara Cara, navel, or blood oranges; or red or yellow grapefruit)

3 cups vanilla ice cream or Brown Sugar–Vanilla Ice Cream (page 187)

Good-quality extra-virgin olive oil

Flaky sea salt

DIY: BEESWAX WRAPS

THERE'S NOT A LOT OF IRONING done around the ranch, but when I do use something besides a branding iron, it's because I'm making beeswax wraps, which are reusable covers for leftovers, sandwiches, and whatever else might need plastic bags or wrap. Made by painting a mixture of beeswax, pine resin, and jojoba oil onto cotton fabric, then ironing it in so that the fabric soaks up the mixture, the wraps become waterproof and tacky enough to stick to themselves. They're a fun family project, and when you have them on hand, you use a lot less plastic and aluminum foil. I make big rounds (about 2 inches larger in diameter than my dinner plates) for storing leftovers, 13-inch squares for wrapping sandwiches, and other various sizes for topping that half-eaten bowl of yogurt, storing the hunk of onion I didn't use, or covering the leftover sauce I can't bear to throw out.

This project makes enough wraps for two kitchens—which means it's perfect if you have a gift to give or if you want to tackle the process with a friend. Start by choosing your fabric, which must be 100 percent cotton to soak up the wax properly, then source the remaining ingredients online. Note that anything that touches the wax, including the bowl you put the wax in and whatever you use to stir the wax mixture, shouldn't be precious, because the mixture is extremely difficult to remove once it dries.

To use the wraps, simply fold them over the top of a plate or bowl, or around a sandwich (they're great for catching drips as you eat!), and the heat from your hands makes the layers of the wrap stick together. But since they need to be washed with cold water so the wax doesn't melt, it's best not to use them to store raw meat.

Note that the combination of wrap sizes below can be cut from two 1-yard pieces of fabric, but if you use smaller fabric pieces, you may not be able to get all eighteen wraps out of them. Either plan your cuts first to be most efficient or buy a little extra fabric just in case. Or only make the sizes that appeal to you most.

Makes at least 18 assorted-size wraps: four 8-inch squares;
four 9-inch squares; four 13-inch squares; two 8-inch rounds;
two 12-inch rounds; two 11-by-15-inch rectangles

➡︎

First, make the beeswax mixture: Put the pellets, pine resin, and jojoba oil in a medium mixing bowl set over a medium saucepan with an inch or so of water in the bottom; the base of the bowl should hover above the water. Place this makeshift double boiler over medium-low heat and cook, stirring frequently with a spatula you don't mind forever donating to this type of project, until the beeswax and resin have melted completely and the mixture is clear, 15 to 20 minutes, adjusting the heat as needed so the water maintains a bare simmer. (You'll notice the wax melts before the resin; keep cooking until the resin has melted completely and no longer forms swirls in the beeswax.) Note that you'll need to either leave the spoon in the bowl as you go or set it on a piece of parchment paper; you don't want to put the hot wax mixture directly on your kitchen counter.

While the mixture melts, set up the waxing station: Fold an old towel in halves or quarters so it covers a stretch of counter (or better yet, a craft table) about 3 feet by 2 feet. Tear off two 2-foot-long pieces of parchment paper and place them on the towel, then tear off four more similar sheets. Place two of the sheets aside, then place two of the sheets on another flat surface, like the counter or the floor, if your kitchen is filling up. (This is where the wax wraps will dry.) Empty the iron of any water, turn off the steam function, and heat to the "high" or "cotton" setting.

Once the wax mixture has melted completely, carefully transfer the double boiler to a trivet or pot holder beside the towel. (The hot water below will keep the wax nice and runny as you work.) Set one of the smaller fabric pieces on top of one of the pieces of parchment on the towel. Dip a clean paintbrush in the wax mixture and paint a thin layer over the entire surface of the fabric, taking care to get the wax all the way to the edges. Top with the second piece of parchment, aligning the layers so no wax creeps out of the parchment (and onto your iron!), and iron thoroughly until you see that the moisture of the wax has melted into the fabric. Carefully remove the top piece of parchment and set it aside, sticky side up, then carefully peel the fabric off the bottom piece of parchment. Wave the fabric around for a moment to cool, then transfer the wax wrap to one of the reserved pieces of parchment to dry. Repeat with the remaining fabric and wax, replacing the top piece of parchment with one of the extras partway through the process if it gets wax on the top side. (You don't want any wax touching the iron.) Starting with smaller fabric pieces and working up toward larger pieces allows the extra wax on the parchment to be incorporated into new pieces as you go. While you work, you can stack the cooled dry wax wraps somewhere else to make room for new hot wraps on the drying area.

2 cups beeswax pellets

⅔ cup pine resin powder or crushed pine resin chunks

2 teaspoons jojoba oil

Old mixing bowl

Medium saucepan

Old rubber spatula or wooden spoon

Parchment paper

Old towel

Iron

Trivet or pot holder

About 2 yards 36-inch-wide assorted 100 percent cotton fabric, washed and dried, trimmed, and cut into desired sizes

New 2-inch paintbrush (a wooden "chip brush" is fine)

Olive oil and paper towel, for cleaning

Scissors

You may wind up with a little of the wax mixture on your fingertips—it comes off easily, but not with water. To remove it, try moistening a paper towel with olive oil and use it to rub off the wax. The same works with any accidental spills!

Once all the wraps are dry, trim away any wayward strings with scissors. The wraps look best as gifts when they're still flat, folded neatly, or rolled together in little bundles and tied with string, but to activate the wax in the wraps and make them effectively tacky, you'll need to scrunch and unscrunch each wrap a few times before using—the heat of your hands will allow them to become sticky like plastic wrap.

TIPS AND TRICKS

- The wax will tint your fabrics a slightly darker shade, so pick colors and patterns that will look good a bit darker.

- If you notice the wax mixture seems to be thickening over time, return the double boiler to low heat and bring the water back to a simmer, then stir for a few minutes, until the mixture thins, and resume your work. (You can also stop mid-project and allow the wax to cool in the bowl, then simply reheat it until liquefied when you're ready to start again.)

- If there are a few wax wraps that seem particularly thick or sticky, transfer some of their wax to another (new) wrap: First, place a fresh piece of fabric between two completed wax wraps. Arrange the fabric sandwich between two pieces of parchment paper, without brushing on additional wax, and iron. The extra wax will transfer to the new fabric. This time, transfer the top and bottom wraps to parchment to dry, and check to make sure the middle layer is completely waxed (and doesn't show any dry spots). Transfer to parchment to cool, or brush any dry spots with additional wax (or rearrange the fabrics and repeat), re-iron, and let dry. Wax wraps work with a lot less wax than you might think, so following this method will allow you to make more wraps.

- If you want to make wax wraps with pieces of fabric larger than your parchment, fold them in half, and iron them folded—the wax still seeps through all of the layers. Make sure there are no dry spots at the fold when you open the wraps.

- Store the wraps at room temperature.

- Wash the wraps in cool or room temperature water with a sponge and regular dish soap, and hang to dry. Always wash your wraps with cold water; hot water will melt or deform the wax.

- As the wraps age with use, you might find their stickiness fades. To renew them, simply layer between parchment, re-iron, and cool as instructed, and they'll be good as new!

A CHRISTMAS FEAST

Menu for 8 to 12

THE CHRISTMAS SEASON STARTS the day after Thanksgiving for us. That's the day the girls head up the mountain by themselves—no parents permitted—to cut down our Christmas tree. The first time they did it years ago, they got impatient waiting for me, so they took it upon themselves to go on their own, and now it's our tradition. I wouldn't have it any other way. They figure out how to navigate the tree through the front door and fit it into the tree stand, then they trim the tree top to bottom with lights and a hodgepodge collection of ornaments.

But no one makes Christmas feel more special than my mom, Jannie. From the fir-wrapped banisters to the candles to the hank-needlepoint stockings, she gets every detail right, which means it's pure joy to walk in on Christmas Eve every year after a long (and sometimes snowy) drive from the ranch down to the Bay Area. My parents always greet us with special cocktails (Shirley Temples for the girls!), and the fun begins: we have a family-wide "Mr. or Mrs. Best Dressed" award (which is really all about the bling), we make a brunch casserole for Christmas morning, and my mom has a tradition of giving the girls matching nightgowns before opening presents on Christmas Eve. Our family has always celebrated with a big cracked-crab dinner. Santa comes afterwards when the adults "hear" the sleigh bells, and all the kids rush downstairs to find their presents.

Christmas Day is more about food than gifts. That night, we gather around the fireplace with drinks and appetizers. For dinner, the sides vary but, without exception, at the center of the table there is a gorgeous prime rib—something we reserve for special occasions and always savor.

MENU TIPS

My mom is the queen of making things ahead so that dinner for a crowd doesn't appear to take much effort at all—but I know better. It's a skill I use often on the ranch for meals too! If you can, make the pickled onions, candied pecans, and vinaigrette for the salad, along with the crab cakes, tartar sauce, and celery root puree, the day before.

A smaller prime rib will serve 10 easily if you're making this entire menu, but the prime rib on its own might only serve 8. Since we usually have about 30 people at our Christmas dinner, we often roast two full-size prime ribs! We use 7-rib cuts that typically weigh in at around 18 to 20 pounds each.

While the meat rests, reheat the crab cakes and serve them as an appetizer, then reheat the celery root puree while you slice the meat.

DURING MY MOTHER'S CHILDHOOD, my grandfather loved to host and cook for big family events. He always served cracked crab with a mayonnaise-based sauce and hot crusty sourdough on Christmas Eve, starting with the fresh crab he'd buy live at the fish market. It doesn't get more San Francisco than that! We still do this every year, with my dad carrying on the tradition. The girls delight in the sight of live crabs in a cooler before dinner, and we always prepare enough to have plenty of leftover crabmeat for a Christmas Day seafood appetizer—like these crab cakes, made with plenty of fresh Dungeness crab. They're the ideal handheld make-ahead bites for a special occasion.

SALTINE-CRUSTED BITE-SIZE CRAB CAKES WITH JALAPEÑO TARTAR SAUCE

Makes 3 dozen crab cakes, plus 1½ cups tartar sauce

Preheat the oven to 425 degrees F. Line a baking sheet with parchment paper and set aside.

To make the crab cakes, in a medium skillet, melt 2 tablespoons of the butter over medium heat until foamy. Add the onion and cook, stirring occasionally, for 3 minutes, until translucent. Add the garlic and stir for about 15 seconds, then transfer the mixture to a medium mixing bowl. Add the crab, ½ cup of the cracker crumbs, the eggs, Old Bay, salt, and pepper, and stir until well blended.

Put the remaining ¾ cup cracker crumbs in a small bowl. Using a tablespoon, form the crab mixture into 36 balls, each about a packed tablespoon's worth. Working with one ball at a time, flatten each into a roughly 1½-inch-wide and ¾-inch-thick disc, then dip it in the cracker crumbs on all sides and transfer to the prepared baking sheet. Repeat with the remaining balls and crumbs. (The crab cakes can be made to this point and refrigerated, covered, for up to 24 hours, or you can freeze them directly on the baking sheet, then pack them into an airtight container and freeze for up to 1 month.)

Brush the crab cakes all over with the remaining 4 tablespoons melted butter, then bake for 15 minutes (or slightly longer from frozen), or until well toasted.

FOR THE CRAB CAKES
6 tablespoons unsalted butter, melted, divided
½ cup finely chopped yellow onion
1 large clove garlic, minced
1 pound fresh Dungeness crabmeat, flaked
1¼ cups saltine cracker crumbs (from about 35 crackers; see Note), divided
2 large eggs, beaten
1½ teaspoons Old Bay seasoning
¾ teaspoon kosher salt
¼ teaspoon freshly ground black pepper

ingredients continue

➤

Meanwhile, make the tartar sauce. In a small mixing bowl, stir together the mayonnaise, jalapeño, onion, cornichons, capers, lemon zest and juice, and salt and pepper to taste until well blended. Cover and refrigerate until ready to serve, or for up to 3 days.

Serve the crab cakes warm or at room temperature, with the tartar sauce dolloped on top or served alongside for dipping. (Cooled crab cakes can be refrigerated for up to 3 days and reheated for 5 minutes in a 425-degree oven before serving.)

NOTE: To make the cracker crumbs, put the saltines in a large ziplock bag, seal it, and use a rolling pin or wine bottle to roll them until well crushed (but not totally powdered).

FOR THE TARTAR SAUCE

1 cup mayonnaise

1 jalapeño (small or large, depending on how much spice you like), finely chopped

2 tablespoons finely chopped yellow onion

1 tablespoon diced cornichons or dill pickles

1 tablespoon capers, finely chopped

Zest and juice of 1 medium lemon (about 1 teaspoon zest plus 2 tablespoons juice)

Kosher salt and freshly ground black pepper

IT TASTES LIKE MULLED WINE and it drinks like mulled wine, but let's call this what it is: a cocktail. Fortified with cognac and amaro (it's the time to break out the good stuff!), this is the ideal holiday starter when everyone's had a long day of travel and last-minute errands. While it seems like two bottles of wine is plenty for eight people, you might want to consider doubling this for a crowd—especially if you plan to relax outdoors for a few hours.

Although a wine's flavor certainly changes when it's heated, don't be tempted to use cheap wine for this. I look for a good pinot noir from our neighbors up in Oregon's Willamette Valley.

HOT SPICED WINE COCKTAILS

Makes 8 cocktails

In a large pot over medium heat, combine ¾ cup of the honey with the cognac, amaro, Cointreau, cinnamon sticks, allspice berries, and cloves. Bring to a gentle simmer and cook for 2 minutes, stirring occasionally, then add the wine and heat, stirring occasionally, until the wine is steaming but not simmering. Add the lemon juice and up to ¼ cup additional honey to taste, and stir. Serve hot, in small mugs, garnished with the orange slices.

To make ahead, let the wine cool completely and then remove the spices so the flavor doesn't get too strong. Reheat before serving.

1 cup honey, divided
½ cup cognac (such as Courvoisier)
½ cup amaro (such as Amaro Nonino or Averna)
1 tablespoon Cointreau
2 cinnamon sticks
1 teaspoon allspice berries
1 teaspoon whole cloves
2 (750-milliliter) bottles dry red wine (such as good-quality pinot noir)
2 tablespoons freshly squeezed lemon juice (from 1 medium lemon)
1 navel orange, halved through its poles and cut into ¼-inch-thick half-moons

EVEN NOW THAT I RAISE AND COOK MEAT FOR A LIVING, my dad, also known as Grampery, is the prime rib maestro at Christmas. We start with one of our gorgeous 28-day-aged prime ribs; when buying your own, look for a lot of thin white veins running through the meat and plenty of white fat rimming the outer edge of the roast. Before roasting, we pack it with a seasoned salt crust, which hardens and browns beautifully as the meat cooks. It lifts right off before serving, like removing a jacket, and leaves the meat not salty but perfectly seasoned. (For cooking a full 7-rib roast, double everything in the recipe except the meat.)

For special occasions, buy the highest grade beef you can find. Fun fact: beef is graded by putting a translucent piece of graph paper over the rib eye; the more squares on the grid that have fat in them, the higher grade the beef receives.

SALT-JACKET PRIME RIB WITH HORSERADISH CRÈME FRAÎCHE

Makes 8 to 10 servings (or 12 to 15 servings for a larger roast), plus about 3 cups crème fraîche

Pat the roast dry with paper towels, and set it bone side up on a baking sheet.

In a large bowl, whisk together the salt, peppercorns, dry mustard, and garlic powder. Add the water and stir until the salt is evenly sandy and begins to clump up a little. Using your hands, spread about one-third of the salt mixture over the small strip of meat next to the rib bones and pack it into a firm, even layer. Carefully turn the roast over and spread the remaining seasoning over the meat and fat, leaving the meaty ends of the roast clean. (It's fine if some of the salt falls off; just do the best you can to create a shell of salt over the entire top of the roast.) Gently rub the exposed ends with your salty hands—you're just seasoning the meat, so you don't want a full crust here. Set aside and let sit at room temperature for 1 hour before roasting.

Meanwhile, make the crème fraîche. In a small mixing bowl, stir together the crème fraîche, sour cream, horseradish to taste, chives, and lemon zest and juice. Season to taste with salt and pepper, cover, and refrigerate until ready to serve, or up to 3 days.

Preheat the oven to 450 degrees F and arrange a rack in the lower third of the oven.

FOR THE ROAST
1 partial (4- to 5-rib) prime rib roast (12 to 14 pounds), or 1 full 7-rib roast (18 to 20 pounds)
3 cups kosher salt
2 tablespoons peppercorn blend (ideally a mix of red, green, black, and white), crushed or very coarsely ground in a mortar and pestle
1 tablespoon dry mustard powder
2 teaspoons garlic powder
¾ cup warm water

FOR THE CRÈME FRAÎCHE
2 cups (16 ounces) crème fraîche
½ cup sour cream
¼ to ½ cup freshly grated horseradish
¼ cup chopped fresh chives
Zest and juice of 1 large lemon (about 1½ teaspoons zest plus 3 tablespoons juice)
Kosher salt and freshly ground black pepper

➡→

Roast the meat for 1 hour, until the salt crust is nicely browned. Reduce the temperature to 300 degrees F, and roast for 2¼ to 3½ hours more (up to 4 hours more for a full 7-rib roast), or until it registers 135 degrees F on an instant-read thermometer inserted into the center of the roast for medium-rare. (The top of the roast will be very dark.)

When the meat is done, remove it from the oven and let it rest for at least 30 minutes, or up to 1 hour. To serve, remove the crust—it should come off in a few big pieces—and gently transfer the meat to a large cutting board, bone sides up. Slice into large slabs between the bones, or carve the meat away from the bones, and cut the resulting roast into thin slices. Serve warm, with the crème fraîche alongside.

NOTE: Because we're fortunate to have a professional-grade dry-ager at home, we always dry-age our prime ribs an additional 14 to 21 days. The dry-aging process concentrates the flavor and adds a wonderful earthiness. If you want to go big, you can purchase dry-aged beef. You can further dry-age a purchased prime rib at home—just be sure to trim it well before cooking.

FIRE-ROASTED MARROW BONES

My parents installed a brick pizza oven in their backyard when Brian and I were married on the property. It still often serves as the centerpiece for our family festivities—especially when the temperature is cooler (as opposed to the 108-degree scorcher our guests endured on our wedding day!). During the holidays, we love roasting marrow bones in it for a unique, easy, indulgent appetizer.

To roast marrow bones, heat a wood-fired oven or grill to between 500 and 550 degrees F. Place as many pipe-cut (open-faced) marrow bones as you need—to get the kind that are cut lengthwise, not across the bone, you may need to have a chat with your butcher—in a cast-iron pan (or two), cut sides up. Grill them for 15 to 20 minutes, depending on their size, or until the centers are spreadably soft. (Some of the fat may pool on the bottom of the pan. Save it for cooking!) To serve, carefully transfer the bones to a platter and sprinkle generously with flaky sea salt. Spread the marrow on toast points and top with Spiced Pickled Red Onions (page 198).

HERE'S A SALAD THAT'S AS FESTIVE as my parents' house during the holidays. With sweet cherries, spicy pecans, piquant blue cheese, and plenty of greens, it's sort of a party in a bowl—and it holds up well, already dressed, on the table, which is always a plus during a long holiday dinner.

SPINACH, KALE, AND DRIED CHERRY SALAD

Makes 12 servings, plus about 2 cups vinaigrette

To make the candied pecans, line a baking sheet with parchment paper, set a wire rack (the gridded kind) on top, and set aside.

In a medium saucepan, combine ½ cup of the sugar with the water and mash with a fork until the sugar is fully moistened. Place the pan over high heat and cook until the sugar dissolves and turns a rich amber color, swirling the pan occasionally but resisting the temptation to stir. (It will take 5 to 7 minutes, but don't rush it. You want a beautiful deep brown color.) Remove the pan from the heat and carefully add the butter, then stir until it melts. Add the pecans, stir to coat completely, and spread them on the wire rack.

In a small bowl, stir together the remaining 1 tablespoon sugar with the salt, cinnamon, and cayenne to taste. Sprinkle this mixture evenly over the pecans and let cool completely.

To make the vinaigrette, in a blender, blend 1 cup of the olive oil, vinegar, Dijon, maple syrup, salt, and pepper until smooth. Season to taste with additional oil (if the dressing is too sharp for your taste), salt, and pepper and set aside.

To assemble the salad, pile the spinach and kale into a large serving bowl and top with the pecans, onions, cherries, and cheese. Dress the salad to taste with the vinaigrette, toss well, and serve. Store any unused vinaigrette in the refrigerator, covered, for up to 1 week.

FOR THE CANDIED PECANS
½ cup plus 1 tablespoon sugar, divided
2 tablespoons water
¼ cup (½ stick) unsalted butter, cubed, at room temperature
8 ounces (about 2 cups) pecan halves
¾ teaspoon kosher salt
¼ teaspoon ground cinnamon
⅛ to ¼ teaspoon cayenne

FOR THE VINAIGRETTE
1 to 1⅓ cups extra-virgin olive oil
½ cup red wine vinegar
1 tablespoon Dijon mustard
1 tablespoon good-quality maple syrup
½ teaspoon kosher salt
¼ teaspoon freshly ground black pepper

FOR THE SALAD
5 ounces baby spinach (about 4 lightly packed cups)
6 packed cups chopped curly green or red kale (from 1 medium bunch or about ¾ pound), stems removed
1 cup Spiced Pickled Red Onions (page 198)
1 cup dried tart or sour cherries
4 ounces blue cheese or gorgonzola, crumbled

MASHED POTATOES ARE A GREAT TRADITIONAL SIDE for prime rib, but why not try something a little different? Celery root—a root vegetable with a rough exterior and a creamy white inside with great fresh celery flavor—makes a perfect partner for rich, juicy beef. You'll feel like you're purchasing a lot of celery root for this, but much of the wild-looking exterior gets trimmed away.

MAKE-AHEAD CELERY ROOT PUREE

Makes 12 servings

Using a small knife, trim away all the roots, brown skin, and light-green parts of each celery root until you're left with just the firm white insides. Cut into 1-inch chunks, transfer to a large pot, add the salt and water to cover, cover with a lid, and bring to a boil over high heat. Reduce the heat to maintain a low simmer and cook, covered, until the celery root is completely soft, about 15 minutes.

Drain the celery root and transfer to a large food processor. Add the butter, lemon zest and juice, and salt and pepper to taste, and process until totally smooth. (If your food processor won't fit everything, you can do this in two batches, dividing the butter and lemon between them.) Serve immediately, or transfer to an oven-proof dish, cool, cover, and refrigerate. To reheat, bake, covered, for about 20 minutes at 350 degrees F, or until warmed through.

8 celery roots (about 8 pounds)
2 tablespoons kosher salt
½ cup (1 stick) unsalted butter, cut into cubes
Zest and juice of 1 large lemon (about 1½ teaspoons zest plus 3 tablespoons juice)
Freshly ground black pepper

THERE AREN'T A LOT OF FRUIT TREES that grow well in our valley, but when we moved to the ranch, we were thrilled to find an apple tree growing well right next to the hay barn. Every year, the girls pick a mini harvest. Any not-quite-perfect fruit goes to the horses or pigs, and the rest goes into the refrigerator for the pies we make all fall. Over the holidays, we always bring apples down to my parents' house and fold them into a version of apple pie with the crunch of Oregon hazelnuts and a dose of cardamom, which together give the pie an almost Scandinavian accent.

While chilling a pie crust is always important, I've found that you can cut corners in the rolling-out process—meaning you can roll out the dough immediately after making it, as long as the dough has time to get good and cold before baking.

CARDAMOM APPLE PIE <u>WITH</u> HAZELNUTS

Makes one 9-inch pie

Make the pie crust as directed. Separate the dough into two roughly equal portions. Working with a floured rolling pin on a lightly floured board, roll each portion into a 12-inch round. Line a baking sheet with parchment paper. Lightly flour each round, stack them on the prepared sheet, and refrigerate for 1 hour. (You can also cover and refrigerate for up to 24 hours.)

To make the filling, in a large bowl, toss together the apples, both sugars, flour, cardamom, cinnamon, and sea salt to blend. Fold in the hazelnuts and set aside.

Remove the dough from the fridge. Fit one round into the bottom of a 9-inch pie pan (the deep-dish kind works best here), allowing the excess dough to hang over the sides. (If you've chilled the dough overnight, you may need to leave it at room temperature for 5 to 10 minutes before it's soft enough to bend into the pan.) Dump the apple mixture into the crust, shaking the apples around as needed to settle them into the pan.

Transfer the second dough round to a large cutting board, and using a large, sharp knife, cut it into 10 roughly 1-inch-thick strips. Brush the interior edge of the fitted bottom crust and the strips lightly with the egg mixture.

1 recipe All-Purpose Double Pie Crust (page 166)
6 large tart, firm apples (such as Cortland, Cox's Orange Pippin, or Granny Smith; about 3 pounds total), peeled, cored, and cut into about 12 wedges each
½ cup granulated sugar
½ cup packed dark brown sugar
2 tablespoons all-purpose flour
1½ teaspoons ground cardamom
½ teaspoon ground cinnamon
½ teaspoon fine sea salt
1 cup roasted, skinned hazelnuts, roughly chopped
1 large egg beaten with 1 tablespoon water

>—→

Transfer the strips to the top of the pie, egg side up, placing the longest strips across the center and the shorter strips toward the edges. You can either place five strips in one direction, then simply layer the remaining five strips in the other direction, or you can scour the internet for instructions on making a lattice-top pie. Gently press the strips into the bottom crust where they meet.

Using scissors or a small, sharp knife, trim the crust to about ½ inch beyond the edge of the pan. Fold the bottom crust over the strips all the way around the pie, then use your fingers or a fork to crimp the edges closed. Brush the edges with the egg mixture, then transfer the pie to a clean parchment-lined baking sheet and refrigerate for another 30 minutes, or up to 4 hours. Reserve the egg wash.

When ready to bake, preheat the oven to 375 degrees F.

Brush the pie all over with another thin layer of egg wash, and bake for 75 to 90 minutes (longer if the pie's been chilling for a while), or until the pie is well browned and the filling bubbles slowly anywhere you can see it. Let the pie cool for at least an hour, or overnight, before serving.

OUR CHRISTMAS TRADITIONS

Our Christmas gift traditions are a little different: Santa visits on Christmas Eve. As soon as dinner is over, the kids are eager to clear the table and do the dishes, since that usually signals a sharp-eyed adult to spot Santa's sleigh. All the kids run upstairs to hide together with a few uncles in the third-floor bedroom while Santa puts presents out—and then the door closes with a "Ho ho ho!" When we hear sleigh bells, everyone rushes down to see what Santa left. We dig into the present pile under the tree, but after that, we're often too exhausted for dessert. Christmas Day is when dessert happens, when we can savor it (with the Brown Sugar–Vanilla Ice Cream on page 187).

DIY: DRIED CITRUS WHEELS

MY GIRLS LIKE TO BE CRAFTY and are each creative in their own way, and they all get excited for our decorating traditions. I'll come home on an October afternoon to find they've carved pumpkins for fun before Halloween, or wake up on a December morning to find them adding holiday lights to our bottle baby barn for a little extra flair. One project we love to do together is making dried citrus wheels, which then become a staple decoration. I watch while the girls cut the citrus into thin slices, and then they are baked until dry. It's really that easy.

The possibilities are almost endless: String them up as garland. Make them the stars of a holiday table runner (page 289). Use paper clips to turn them into ornaments. Tuck them under a whole ham or turkey as a pretty garnish. Pair them with paper cards and some twine to make name tags for a dinner party. You could make about four batches and string the citrus together on yarn to make a pretty wreath, or just a single batch to decorate a few store-bought wreaths. Cut them in half and use them as roof shingles on a gingerbread house. They even make a fun cocktail garnish!

You can use any citrus you'd like for these. Just note that larger wheels will take longer to dry, and the thicker you cut the fruit, the longer it will take too. Using a mandoline will give you the best thin, even slices, with that stained-glass look, but even thicker slices cut less perfectly will look beautiful.

Makes 3 to 4 dozen wheels

Line 2 baking sheets with 2 layers of paper towels each. Arrange the orange slices on the towels, then top with another 2 layers of paper towels, and let sit for 15 minutes. Press down gently with flat hands to press out any extra juices, then transfer the oranges (with towels) to a flat surface to empty the baking sheets.

Preheat the oven to 200 degrees F. Line the same baking sheets with parchment paper.

Move the citrus wheels to the parchment paper, spreading them out in a single layer, then sprinkle evenly with the sugar. (They will shrink during baking, so it's OK if they overlap a little.) Bake for 4 to 7 hours (again, this will really depend on the size and thickness of your slices), flipping every hour or so, until the wheels are shrunken, a few shades darker in color, and dried. (The fully dried citrus will still bend when they're warm, but they'll stiffen and crisp as they cool.)

Cool completely, then use as desired. Store completed dried citrus in an airtight container for up to 3 months.

4 medium oranges (or any combination of oranges, lemons, limes, and grapefruit), ends trimmed, sliced ¼- to ⅛-inch thick, seeds removed
1 tablespoon sugar

SPRING IS ALL ABOUT RENEWAL AROUND THE RANCH. While we're still heating our home with wood in March, come April, our valley bursts into life, almost overnight, right around the time Maisie and I celebrate our birthdays. As the weather warms, the ewes and rams need a trim, which means scheduling our annual sheep-shearing weekend.

In April, the grass season also starts. We get ready to start irrigating again, fixing broken pipes, checking on all our well systems, and making sure our irrigation pivots and wheel lines are in good working order after the harsh winter. The first day we let the cows back onto the pasture is glorious. They literally jump through the grass when they first see it, bounding like animals a fraction of their size. Sometimes I just stand in the middle of the pasture to listen to them chew.

May, one of my favorite months on the ranch, is when we begin having visitors again: we open up our big outdoor kitchen that sits amid the oak grove on the hill behind our upper cattle pastures and the horse pastures. Friends and relatives often come to visit Camp, as we call it, staying in the rugged but well-appointed wall tents we put up once it's warm enough to sleep outdoors. They are usually excited to wake up early, do morning chores with Brian, dig with me in the garden, and generally lend a hand around the ranch. It's a great time to remember how much we appreciate having friends around—especially when it means we can feed them ribs and potato salad outside at the end of a long day.

FIRESIDE FEAST

Menu for 6

AS RANCHERS, "DATE NIGHT" USUALLY MEANS HAVING A CHORE BEER together while we finish up things on the ranch in the evening. Brian and I count on this time when it's usually just the two of us. It's an opportunity for us to talk about how things went that day and what's on our to-do list for the next.

Before we moved to the ranch, we'd get a babysitter and go out to dinner at our favorite steakhouse for a "real" date night as often as we could. We still find time to get away when we can, but often we just decide to up our date-night game at home—typically centered around what we cook, which is always enough food for the whole family but special enough that Brian and I want to enjoy a nice bottle of wine by the woodstove or up at Camp after the girls run off to feed bottle babies or play in the Little House. Rack of lamb fits the bill because we reserve it for special occasions (usually when my parents are on the ranch). What I like most is that while a rack of lamb is elegant and delicious, it's also relatively easy to prepare. When it's paired with potatoes and asparagus that roast in the oven at the same temperature—and a dessert that can be whirled up in the blender—the result is a special meal that offers the best of all worlds.

MENU TIPS

The components of this dinner feel special and may sound more complicated than my usual approach, but they come together without too much time or effort. Roast the potatoes and the lamb together on the same baking sheet, then put the asparagus in while the lamb rests. If you're making this for a date night for two, you can simply halve the recipes for the lamb, potatoes, and asparagus. And if you really want to stay on theme, make some homemade candles—or have your kids do it for you!

AFTER THE WINTER, when we spend a lot of time focusing on our lambs and making sure any animals who aren't born strong get nursed well, the spring feels like a good time to celebrate our flock's strength. Every year after our first harvest, we remember why we chose Navajo-Churro sheep: the breed is a natural chef's choice because it has good lamb flavor without tasting overly gamey. It's a huge hit with lamb lovers, but we've also converted many people who swore they'd never liked lamb before they tasted ours. We feed our animals high-quality alfalfa and pasture grasses, which is one reason the resulting meat tastes so good.

Lamb cooks quickly and evenly and is naturally packed with flavor. Rack of lamb is, perhaps counterintuitively, something I think of as a fast, easy dinner. Even when you french the bones and dress it up with mustardy herb-packed bread crumbs, like I do here, your work is done before the oven's finished heating. But because it makes a statement when it hits the table, it doubles as date-night-at-home fare, or a standout centerpiece when you've invited friends for dinner.

If you've never frenched lamb, you can always have a butcher do this for you. To do it yourself: Make a cut through the layer of fat that covers the meat, running perpendicular to the bones about 4 inches from their tips, across the entire length of the rack. Cut and peel away the fat that covers the bones. Then, using a small, sharp knife, cut away the fat and tissue between each bone.

ROSEMARY–DIJON ROASTED RACK OF LAMB

Makes 6 servings

Preheat the oven to 425 degrees F.

Place the lamb on a baking sheet and season all sides with salt and pepper. Turn the racks fat side up.

In a medium mixing bowl, stir together the bread crumbs, olive oil, rosemary, Dijon, 1½ teaspoons salt, and 1 teaspoon pepper until evenly moist. Pat half of the mixture in an even layer over one of the racks, covering all of the lamb except the bones and tossing any crumbs that escape back on top. Repeat with the remaining mixture and the second rack of lamb.

Roast the lamb for 25 to 30 minutes, until the bread crumbs are evenly brown and the meat registers 125 degrees F for medium-rare or 135 degrees F for medium on an instant-read thermometer. Let the lamb rest for 10 minutes, then cut the rack into chops and serve them topped with the crispy bread crumbs.

2 (2½- to 3-pound) racks of
   lamb, frenched (or not)
Kosher salt and freshly ground
   black pepper
1 cup plain bread crumbs
½ cup extra-virgin olive oil
⅓ cup finely chopped fresh
   rosemary (or thyme or sage)
¼ cup Dijon mustard

FOR A SIMPLE SIDE DISH with plenty of color, roast new potatoes with a big shower of fresh herbs. If you're making the Rosemary-Dijon Roasted Rack of Lamb on page 90, you can do double duty and face the two racks toward each other, so the bones cross, and snuggle the foil packet right underneath the bones. The potatoes can continue cooking while the lamb rests, if needed. You can also make these potatoes right over a fire or on the grill, turning the foil packet every so often for even cooking.

FOIL-WRAPPED NEW POTATOES WITH OLIVE OIL AND HERB FLURRY

Makes 6 servings

Preheat the oven to 425 degrees F.

On a large sheet of heavy-duty aluminum foil, drizzle the potatoes with the olive oil, season with kosher salt and pepper, and toss to coat thoroughly. Wrap the foil tightly around the potatoes, then place them on a baking sheet and roast for 30 to 40 minutes, or until the potatoes are completely tender. Leave the potatoes wrapped in foil until just before serving, then transfer the foil to a bowl, open the package, and drizzle the potatoes with a little more olive oil, shower with the herbs, and sprinkle with a little sea salt.

1½ pounds small (about 1-inch) new potatoes

2 tablespoons extra-virgin olive oil, plus more for drizzling

Kosher salt and freshly ground black pepper

¼ cup roughly chopped mixed fresh herbs (such as chives, dill, tarragon, parsley, or basil)

Flaky sea salt

MY MOM GREW UP IN WATSONVILLE, California, south of the Bay Area in the Pajaro Valley, where asparagus farms thrive. Asparagus was also a staple at my family's dinner table—and often just served with mayonnaise for dipping, which my own girls also love. My Instagram followers are always very clearly on Team Mayo or Team No Way every time I share photos of the kids eating asparagus this way, but it's our favorite.

When we want to level up a little, though, we roast asparagus and top it with fried lemons made by just cooking thinly sliced lemon over high heat in a little bit of olive oil. The rind softens and sweetens as it cooks, so you can eat the entire thing. You can use the same method for any vegetable that tastes great with a squeeze of lemon—try broccoli, green beans, cauliflower, snap peas, or zucchini.

ASPARAGUS WITH FRIED LEMON AND GARLIC

Makes 6 servings

Preheat the oven to 425 degrees F.

Pile the asparagus into a 9-by-13-inch baking dish and drizzle with 2 tablespoons of the olive oil, then season with salt and pepper. Toss the spears to coat evenly, then spread them out in a roughly even layer. Roast for 8 to 10 minutes, or until crisp-tender.

Meanwhile, slice the lemon in half lengthwise, pick out any visible seeds, and set aside one-half for later. Slice the remaining half into ⅛-inch-thick half-moons, removing any seeds.

Heat a large skillet over medium-high heat. Add the remaining 2 tablespoons olive oil, and when the oil is shimmering, carefully add the lemon slices in a single layer, then toss in the garlic. Cook undisturbed for about 1 minute, or until the lemon slices turn dark brown.

Remove the pan from the heat, flip the lemon slices and garlic, and let them continue cooking off the heat while the asparagus finish cooking.

When the asparagus are ready, squeeze the reserved lemon half over the fried lemon slices, then scrape the entire lemon-garlic mixture over the asparagus and serve immediately.

2 pounds asparagus, ends trimmed
4 tablespoons extra-virgin olive oil, divided
Kosher salt and freshly ground black pepper
1 large lemon, ends trimmed
2 cloves garlic, peeled and smashed

I LOVE A SOLID DESSERT RECIPE that I can put in my back pocket for whenever I need it. This is one of those—a recipe that's simple enough to memorize (because it's equal parts of each main ingredient), super quick to make, and flexible for any time of year. Clafoutis (pronounced kla-foo-TEE) may have an intimidating French name, but at heart it's a rustic eggy dessert that's right at home on our ranch. Essentially a custard made with milk, cream, sugar, eggs, and whatever fruit you have on hand, clafoutis traditionally features cherries (with pits!), but it's infinitely adaptable. My family loves it, and I bet yours will too.

While rhubarb is my favorite version in the spring, I make clafoutis year-round with any fresh berries, sliced stone fruits (cherries, nectarines, or plums), apples, or pears I have on hand—you just need enough fruit to cover the bottom of the pan. Clafoutis also makes a delicious breakfast!

RHUBARB CLAFOUTIS

Makes 6 servings

Preheat the oven to 350 degrees F and position a rack in the center of the oven.

Generously grease an 8-inch square (or similar) baking dish with butter, then scatter the rhubarb across the bottom of the dish.

In a blender, blend the milk, cream, granulated sugar, flour, eggs, vanilla, and salt on high speed for 30 seconds. Pour the batter directly into the baking dish, over and around the rhubarb, then bake for about 45 minutes, or until puffed in the center and lightly browned.

Dust the clafoutis with confectioners' sugar just before serving warm or at room temperature.

Unsalted butter, for greasing the pan
½ pound rhubarb (2 stalks), sliced into ½-inch pieces (about 2 cups)
¾ cup whole milk
¾ cup heavy cream
¾ cup granulated sugar
¾ cup all-purpose flour
4 large eggs
1 tablespoon vanilla extract
¼ teaspoon kosher salt
Confectioners' sugar, for dusting

DIY: ROLLED BEESWAX CANDLES

I LOVE THE SOFT GLOW beeswax candles give off, and of course how the wax melts so dramatically over the course of a long, slow dinner. The best part? They're really easy to make. You just need two main ingredients: preformed sheets of beeswax and candle wicking, which is essentially string with a special weave to it. Wrap the sheets around the wicking, and you've got candles (or gifts!) in no time. And because there's no melting involved, they're easy for kids to make with minimal supervision so you can focus on cooking.

You can purchase the beeswax sheets and wicking online. We use natural-colored beeswax the most, but it's also fun to make colored candles for holiday gifts.

Makes 20 (8-inch) taper candles or 40 (6-inch) twisted taper candles or 10 (4-inch) pillar candles, or a combination of the three

- 10 (8-by-16-inch) natural-colored beeswax sheets, any paper removed
- Up to 10 yards of square-braid (#1 size) cotton candle wicking
- Ruler
- Pencil
- Scissors
- Hair dryer

First, cut and roll the candles based on type.

TO MAKE TAPER CANDLES: Place one beeswax sheet on a work surface with one long side closest to you. Use a ruler and a pencil to draw a vertical line that separates the piece into two 8-inch squares. Cut the sheet with scissors into equal pieces along the line.

Working with one sheet at a time, roll the candles. First, cut a 9-inch piece of wicking. Line the wicking up parallel with the side of the sheet closest to you, about ¼ inch from the bottom of the sheet, and allow about ½ inch of wick to hang off either end. Gently press the wick into the beeswax to encourage it to stick, then fold the bottom edge of the sheet over the wick to seal it in place. (It's OK if the wax breaks a little here, but if you're working in a cool place, the wax may be too stiff—you can use a hair dryer on low heat to slightly soften the entire sheet of wax for about 30 seconds.) Once the wick is covered, roll the entire beeswax sheet into a tight tube around the wick, keeping the ends aligned as you roll.

TO MAKE TWISTED TAPER CANDLES: Place one beeswax sheet on a work surface with one long side closest to you. Use a ruler and a pencil to draw a vertical line that separates the piece into two 8-inch squares. Cut the sheet with scissors into equal pieces along the line.

Working with one square at a time, use a pencil to make a mark 1 inch in from the bottom left-hand corner of the sheet on the edge closest to you. Make another mark 1 inch in from the top right-hand corner of the sheet on the opposite parallel edge. Use a ruler as a guide to draw a line between the two marks, then cut along the line with scissors so the square is divided into two triangles, each with one corner that doesn't quite come to a point.

→

Place the triangle on the right in front of you, then flip the triangle on the left so it looks the same. (The slopes of each triangle should slant downward and to the left, with the unpointed corner of each triangle on the upper right-hand side.)

Working with one triangle at a time, roll the candles. First, cut an 8-inch piece of wicking. Line the wicking up parallel with the side of the sheet closest to you, about ¼ inch from the bottom of the sheet, and allow about ½ inch of wick to hang off either end. Gently press the wick into the beeswax to encourage it to stick, then fold the bottom edge of the sheet over the wick to seal it in place. (It's OK if the wax breaks a little here, but if you're working in a cold place, the wax may be too stiff— you can use a hair dryer on low heat to slightly soften the entire sheet of wax for about 30 seconds.) Once the wick is covered, roll the entire beeswax triangle into a tight tube around the wick, keeping the right side aligned as you roll. (The rolling action will create a twisting pattern.)

TO MAKE PILLAR CANDLES: Place one beeswax sheet on a work surface with one long side closest to you. Use a ruler and a pencil to draw a horizontal line that separates the piece into two 16-by-4-inch rectangles. Cut the sheet with scissors into equal pieces along the line. (If the sheets are slightly wider than 8 inches, which sometimes happens, you may need to trim them down to wind up with two 4-inch strips.)

Working with one rectangle at a time, roll the candle. First, cut one 5-inch piece of wicking. Turn the sheet so that one short side is closest to you. Line the wicking up parallel with the short side, about ¼ inch from the bottom of the sheet, and allow about ½ inch of wick to hang off either end. Gently press the wick into the beeswax to encourage it to stick, then fold the bottom edge of the sheet over the wick to seal it in place. (It's OK if the wax breaks a little here, but if you're working in a cold place, the wax may be too stiff—you can use a hair dryer on low heat to slightly soften the entire sheet of wax for about 30 seconds.) Once the wick is covered, roll the beeswax sheet into a tight tube around the wick, keeping the ends aligned as you roll, until all but about 2 inches of beeswax is rolled. Place the second rectangle over the end of the first sheet so it overlaps the first by about ½ inch and effectively makes it twice as long. Continue rolling until you reach the end of the second sheet.

TO FINISH CANDLES: Once all the candles are rolled, use your thumb to gently press the exposed edge of the beeswax sheet into the layer of wax below, working down the length of each candle until the entire edge is sealed shut. (For twisted candles, only seal the seam on the lower portion of the candle, where it's sturdier.) Once the seam is complete, trim the wick to ¼ inch on both ends. Choose which end of the candle you want to be the top. At the other end, press the wick into the wax, then stand up the candle on a firm surface, and press the candle down gently to give it a flat bottom. The candles will burn for 30 to 60 minutes.

EASTER SUNDAY SUPPER

Menu for 8

WHEN MY SISTER, TWO BROTHERS, AND I WERE GROWING UP in the Bay Area, my mom made Easter an extra-special celebration. There was always an egg hunt, but she also organized lots of creative Easter games and contests. (We are a little competitive around here!) We did an egg-drop contest, taking turns dropping our egg-holding contraptions from the third-floor balcony to see whose setup could prevent their egg from cracking when it landed. We had egg-decorating contests using vivid Ukrainian dyes and melted wax for layers of color. We also played the Greek Easter–inspired egg-cracking game with red-dyed eggs: we'd each hold what we deemed to be the strongest hard-boiled egg we had found in the hunt and bump its ends against the others' eggs, hoping to hold the last remaining uncracked egg at the end. My mom had a bottomless box of silly prizes—the same kinds of things you'd put in a Christmas stocking—and we got to pick from it if we won.

We try to get to my parents' house for Easter some years, and my mom still does all the same fun games for the young cousins. But if we are on the ranch, it means Easter looks a little different. We don't get to pause animal care for holidays, but we still color eggs to hide and make the egg-topped Easter buns my mom made and usually have a special dinner. Instead of rubbing a ham with beer, dry mustard powder, and honey—my dad's annual tradition when I was young—we usually prepare some sort of pork roast and cook it outdoors on a spit or on the barbecue, even if it's cold or we get a late-season snowfall. We always save room for dessert too. I hope my girls look forward to Easter every year as much as I did.

MENU TIPS

This is a menu that requires a lot of cooking time, so pace it well. Dye the eggs a few days ahead. If you'd like, you can make the aioli for the artichokes a day or two in advance also. Cook the pavlovas and their strawberry topping the night before or the morning of serving. Bake the buns and steam the artichokes just before you roast the pork so they're both still warmish around suppertime. Add the carrots to the oven midway through the pork's cooking time. (The carrots can be served warm or at room temperature.)

For a simpler meal, skip the artichokes and bread, and replace them with Foil-Wrapped New Potatoes with Olive Oil and Herb Flurry (page 92), which can be added to the oven to cook while the pork roasts and cools.

WE ARE HUGE ARTICHOKE EATERS. My mom grew up next to Castroville, California, the so-called artichoke capital of the world, and my grandpa knew many of the farmers. He'd literally cut the artichokes fresh from the fields and bring them home when my mom was younger, though we got them from the grocery store most of the time. Either way, steaming artichokes was a skill all of us four kids loved to take on to help with dinner.

Which is all to say that my girls have the same love for sharing a good steamed artichoke. They know the heart is the best part and that you can't eat an artichoke without something to dip it in. (See How to Eat an Artichoke on page 108.)

While mayonnaise is our standard dip, a punchy aioli is even better. This recipe is more of a faux-oli, really: it calls for store-bought mayonnaise that is amped up with olive oil, fresh lemon juice, and the tart, salty flavor of preserved lemons. (Look for preserved lemons in glass jars near the pickles and olives in a large grocery store.)

ARTICHOKES <u>WITH</u> PRESERVED-LEMON AIOLI

Makes 4 artichokes, plus about 2 cups aioli

Fill a large pot with 1 inch of water and fit it with a steamer insert. (Alternatively, you can wad up a few balls of aluminum foil, put them in the water, and balance a heatproof plate on them just above the surface of the water.) Bring the water to a boil over high heat. Trim 1 inch off the pointy top of each artichoke, and cut off the stems so the artichokes can sit upright. Place the artichokes in the steamer, reduce the heat to low, cover, and steam until a leaf pulled from the side of the choke comes out easily when you tug on it, or until a skewer can pierce the center of the artichoke without much resistance, 30 to 40 minutes (up to 60 minutes for larger chokes). Remove the artichokes and set aside to cool.

While they cook, make the aioli: In a small mixing bowl, whisk together the mayonnaise, olive oil, lemon juice, preserved lemon, garlic, salt, and pepper. Taste and adjust the seasoning as needed. (For a super smooth aioli, you could whirl the ingredients in a food processor until silky and chill for at least 1 hour before serving.) The aioli can be made up to 3 days ahead; refrigerate, covered, until ready to serve.

Serve the artichokes warm or at room temperature with the aioli for dipping.

4 globe artichokes
1½ cups mayonnaise
3 tablespoons extra-virgin olive oil
3 tablespoons freshly squeezed lemon juice (from 1 large lemon)
1 small preserved lemon, halved, seeds removed, finely chopped
1 clove garlic, minced
1¼ teaspoons kosher salt
½ teaspoon ground white pepper

HOW TO EAT AN ARTICHOKE

Artichokes look a little prehistoric with all of those protective spines, so it's no wonder people are intimidated by them—and it's not often we need to be taught how to eat something. They seem to be a lot more common on the West Coast, though. I remember my East Coast college roommates coming to visit and my mom serving a big plate of artichokes. They had never seen one before and didn't know how to go about eating it!

Once the artichokes are cooked, start by pulling a leaf out. (The technical term for a leaf is a "bract.") On the inside of the non-pointy end, there's a nugget of tender flesh. Put this soft end of the leaf in your mouth, concave side down, then pull the leaf back out with your teeth closed around it, scraping the flesh off the leaf with your bottom teeth. Try another bract with the flesh dipped in aioli—or even just plain mayo!

When you've removed all the outer leaves and eaten the flesh from them, you'll be left with just the artichoke's center. This contains arguably the best part—the heart—hidden beneath an inedible part. To get to the heart, remove any white-and-purple leaves to uncover the bed of furry white hairs. This is called the choke. Cut the artichoke in half vertically through the center to reveal a bed of soft flesh under the choke, which is the heart. Using your fingers, pick away all of the hairy choke so that you're left with only the heart. (You may need to rinse the hairs off as they can be sticky.) Cut the heart into quarters or eighths, dip, and enjoy!

WHILE PRIME CUTS OF MEAT (like rack of lamb, beef tenderloin, and prime rib) usually steal the show at big family gatherings, there are other lesser-known cuts that make beautiful, delicious centerpieces for just a fraction of the cost. Take a pork top loin roast, for example: covered with a simple spice mixture (like our M5 Spice Rub on page 21), top loin (also called a boneless loin roast) is a lean, sliceable roast that can be on the table in about an hour. But with a little more effort—say, stuffing the pork with lightly caramelized onions, spinach, herbs, and feta—you get a show-stopping meal that's also really fun to cook. This is a great recipe for older kids who are confident cooks but haven't tried more formal meals, because no matter how precise the pork cut or how much of the stuffing falls out, the roast looks gorgeous and tastes delicious (just don't overcook it!).

You can use this recipe as a blueprint for whatever stuffing you can dream up: Use kale or collards instead of the spinach. Add a layer of thinly sliced prosciutto or chopped kalamata olives or sundried tomatoes. Substitute blue cheese for the feta. And if you'd prefer to use a cut with a little more fat, substitute pork shoulder for the top loin roast.

Note: You'll need five roughly 2-foot-long pieces of kitchen string to tie around the pork.

STUFFED PORK ROAST <u>WITH</u> SPINACH AND FETA

Makes 8 servings

Preheat the oven to 425 degrees F. Position an oven rack a third of the way from the bottom of the oven.

Heat a large skillet over medium heat. When hot, add 1 tablespoon of the olive oil and the onion, and cook and stir until soft and evenly brown, about 10 minutes, decreasing the heat if the onions begin to get too dark. Add the garlic and oregano, and season with salt and pepper. Cook until the garlic is fragrant, about 1 minute, then add the spinach, season again, and cook, stirring frequently, until all liquid has evaporated from the spinach, another 2 to 3 minutes. Add ½ cup of the wine and the broth, and simmer until the liquid has evaporated, another 5 minutes or so. Remove from the heat and stir in the bread crumbs. Set aside to cool.

Meanwhile, prepare the pork for stuffing in one of two ways: For a simpler stuffed roast, cut the roast nearly in half lengthwise, keeping one long side intact so that it opens up like a book with the

5 tablespoons extra-virgin olive oil, divided

1 medium yellow onion, halved and thinly sliced

2 large cloves garlic, minced

2 tablespoons chopped fresh oregano, divided

Kosher salt and freshly ground black pepper

1 (10-ounce) package frozen cut spinach, thawed and drained of any excess liquid

1 cup dry white wine, divided

½ cup beef bone broth

⅓ cup plain bread crumbs

1 (4-pound) boneless top loin pork roast, strings removed

1 tablespoon finely chopped fresh thyme

1 cup (about 4 ounces) crumbled feta

fatty half as its cover. This will result in a roast with a stripe of filling inside. For a butterflied roast (with the filling in a spiral), once the roast is splayed open in half, make two more cuts parallel to the cutting board to halve each open half of the roast again, starting a third of the way toward each edge from the centerline of the opened roast and cutting the meat in half again parallel to the cutting board almost all the way to the outer long sides, again keeping the long sides intact. You should end up with a roast that opens like a four-paneled brochure. Using a heavy skillet, pound the meat to an even thickness (about ½ to ¾ inch thick, depending on the size of the roast).

Season the entire roast inside and out with salt and pepper and the thyme, then close the roast back up so the fattiest part ends up on top.

To stuff the meat, arrange five 2-foot-long pieces of kitchen string at equal intervals (each about 2 inches apart) on a clean work surface. Center the closed roast perpendicular to the strings, with the fat side up, then open the roast and press the stuffing into the inside (on the bottom half, if you sliced it once, or across the entire inside, if you butterflied it), leaving a 1-inch border all the way around so the filling has room to spread when you roll it up. Scatter the feta over the stuffing and gently press it down. Close the roast again, fat side up, gently rolling it into a spiral ending with the fatty top (if you butterflied it). Tie the five strings snugly around the meat and trim away any extra string.

Smear 2 tablespoons of the olive oil across the bottom of a heavy roasting pan. Transfer the pork roast to the pan, drizzle with the remaining 2 tablespoons olive oil, and pour the remaining ½ cup wine around the roast.

Roast for 55 to 75 minutes for a top loin roast, or until the center registers 135 degrees F for medium-rare or 145 degrees F for well-done on an instant-read thermometer. Remove from the oven and let rest for 10 minutes, then cut into ¾-inch to 1-inch slabs and serve hot, drizzled with the pan juices.

THIS CRUNCHY DILLED VERSION OF TRADITIONAL GREMOLATA—an Italian topping made with parsley, garlic, and lemon zest—gives simple roasted carrots, our girls' favorite side dish, a great punch. For an elegant but easy spin on this, make the dish with rainbow carrots, which present especially well. You can roast the carrots on the top rack while the pork (page 109) is in the oven, or make them ahead and serve at room temperature.

ROASTED CARROTS <u>WITH</u> DILL–ALMOND GREMOLATA

Makes 8 servings

Preheat the oven to 425 degrees F.

Cut the carrots in half lengthwise (or into quarters if they're huge), then toss them on a baking sheet with 2 tablespoons of the olive oil and plenty of salt and pepper. Spread them into an even layer and roast for about 30 minutes (less for smaller or younger carrots, more for larger carrots), or until browned and soft.

Meanwhile, finely chop the garlic on a large cutting board, then add the almonds, parsley, dill, and lemon zest to the board. Chop everything together until fine, then transfer the mixture to a small mixing bowl and stir in the lemon juice and remaining tablespoon of olive oil. When the carrots are done, spoon the gremolata on top and toss the carrots to mix it in. Pile the carrots onto a serving platter, shower with sea salt and more pepper, and serve.

2 pounds carrots, trimmed and well scrubbed

3 tablespoons extra-virgin olive oil, divided

Kosher salt and freshly ground black pepper

1 clove garlic

¼ cup toasted slivered almonds

¼ cup fresh flat-leaf parsley leaves

¼ cup fresh dill fronds

Zest and juice of 1 large lemon (about 1½ teaspoons zest plus 3 tablespoons juice)

Flaky sea salt

MY MOM IS IRISH AND CROATIAN, which means that along with a lot of Eastern European Easter traditions (such as the Greek egg-cracking game, page 105), she grew up with a special recipe for Easter egg breads. While her family made them plain, she began baking them with pretty dyed eggs nestled into the dough, which we try to do every year to keep the tradition alive. I love that while some of our traditions are essentially written in stone, many of them (like these breads) evolve from year to year. For example, some years I forgo the super vibrant Ukrainian egg dye and instead opt for experimenting with the more muted colors of naturally dyed eggs, which I make using foods like turmeric, red cabbage, beets, onion skins, and hibiscus flowers.

If you'll use Naturally Dyed Easter Eggs (page 117) for the breads, make them before starting the dough so they'll be ready when it's time to form the breads.

EASTER EGG BREADS

Makes 8 breads

In the bowl of a stand mixer fitted with the paddle attachment, whisk together the warm water and yeast and set aside for about 5 minutes, or until the mixture becomes foamy.

In a small saucepan over medium heat, combine ½ cup of the half-and-half with the butter cubes. Heat until the cream bubbles around the edges, then remove from the heat and let sit, stirring occasionally, until the butter is fully melted.

Add 1 cup of the flour, the 2 eggs, sugar, and salt to the mixer bowl and mix on low until combined. Add the cream mixture and 2 more cups of flour, and mix again on low speed until no white streaks remain.

Switch to the dough hook, add another ½ cup of flour, and turn the machine on low speed until the flour is incorporated. Finally, add only as much of the remaining ½ cup flour as needed, adding just until the dough starts to pull away from the sides and bottom of the bowl. (It won't clean the bowl completely.) Increase the speed to medium and knead the dough for 1 minute, stopping as needed to pull the dough down and off the dough hook.

Grease a medium mixing bowl with the olive oil. Add the dough and turn it to coat all sides of the dough. Cover with a kitchen towel and let the dough rise at room temperature until tripled in size, about 2 hours.

½ cup warm water

1½ teaspoons active dry yeast

½ cup plus 1 teaspoon half-and-half, divided

¼ cup (½ stick) unsalted butter, cubed, at room temperature

3½ to 4 cups all-purpose flour, divided, plus more for forming the dough

2 large eggs plus 1 large egg yolk

3 tablespoons sugar

½ teaspoon kosher salt

2 teaspoons extra-virgin olive oil

8 hard-cooked eggs (dyed, if desired)

➤

Punch the dough down to deflate it and transfer to a clean counter or large board. Pat the dough into a roughly even layer. (The dough will be slightly sticky but shouldn't require dusting.) Using a bench scraper or large knife, cut the dough into eight equal pieces (each weighing about 4 ounces).

Line a baking sheet with parchment paper and set it near your work space.

Using your hands, roll each piece of dough into a 12-inch-long snake. Set the dough aside to rest for about 5 minutes.

Cut each snake crosswise into two equal pieces and roll each piece into a 10-inch-long snake, so you have a total of sixteen snakes. You can pull and squeeze as needed here; because the buns will rise again, it's OK if they are a little lumpy at this point. Let the dough rest again for 5 minutes.

To form a bun, place two dough snakes on a work surface and pinch their ends together on one side. Twist the two snakes over one another repeatedly until you reach the end, then press the two ends together to form a circle. (It will look like a twisted bagel.) Transfer the dough circle to the prepared baking sheet and press the ends together firmly, then place one hard-boiled egg in the center, pointed end up. Repeat with the remaining dough and eggs, spacing the buns evenly across the baking sheet.

Cover loosely with a clean kitchen towel and let the dough rise at room temperature for 45 minutes, or until the buns look puffy and have risen enough to touch or almost touch each other.

About 15 minutes before the dough has finished rising, preheat the oven to 350 degrees F and position a rack in the center of the oven. In a small bowl, whisk together the egg yolk with the remaining teaspoon half-and-half.

Just before baking, brush every surface of the buns gently with a thin layer of the egg wash, avoiding the hard-boiled eggs. (Take your time; any big drips will look like scrambled eggs on the buns.)

Bake for about 30 minutes, or until the tops are golden brown. Remove the buns from the oven and transfer them to a wire rack to cool for about 20 minutes, gently separating them if necessary. Serve warm or at room temperature. Wrap any cooled buns well and store at room temperature for up to 3 days.

NOTE: As you might imagine, having four girls in the house means that a lot of braiding happens. If you want, you can give these a braided look instead of twists: Divide each dough eighth into three pieces, rather than two, then roll each piece into a 10-inch snake and braid the dough instead of twisting it.

DIY: NATURALLY DYED EASTER EGGS

BEFORE WE EVEN MOVED TO THE RANCH, we celebrated one Easter there as a family right after we bought the property. The girls were tiny. We hid eggs up on the hill behind the houses, and as they ventured out to look for them, the hunt turned into an afternoon of exploration around the ranch. The girls discovered the bridge over the irrigation ditch and new kinds of trees to climb and craggy rocks with built-in hiding spots. I'll always remember that Easter as the first time we felt at home on the ranch.

Today our Easter egg hunts are much more competitive and often include multiple families. Some years we add scavenger hunts, complete with clues taped to trees up and down the mountain that the kids have to search for on horseback or quads—obviously with prizes at stake. And every year, we love to dye eggs. Now we turn it into a bit of a science experiment, soaking steamed eggs in various homemade dyes to see what colors we can coax out of nature if we aren't going for the Ukrainian powder dyes I love for their extra vibrant and immediate colors. White eggs usually take the natural dyes better, but you can get some interesting shades with brown, blue, or green farm eggs too. For a sunny mustard hue, I add ground turmeric to the water. Beets make a good pinkish purple, of course. Surprisingly, adding red cabbage yields eggs that are a beautiful deep blue, and brown onion skins turn eggs red. The best secret to a striking black color is dried hibiscus flowers.

Makes 2 dozen dyed eggs

To steam the eggs, fill a large pot with a steamer basket and about 1 inch of water and bring to a boil over high heat. Gently place the eggs in the basket, cover, and steam over medium heat for 10 to 15 minutes, depending on whether you like the yolks dark and fudgy or fully set. (Alternatively, you can steam them for 5 to 7 minutes on a rack in a multicooker on high pressure with 1 cup of water in the bottom.) Immediately transfer the eggs to a bowl of ice-cold water to cool for 10 minutes.

In a small saucepan, combine the cabbage and 3 cups water. Bring to a boil over high heat, then reduce to a simmer and cook for 30 minutes. Remove from the heat, stir in 1 tablespoon of the vinegar, and let cool for 1 hour. Gently submerge 4 eggs into the liquid and refrigerate overnight.

24 large white eggs
¼ head red cabbage, thinly sliced
5 tablespoons distilled white vinegar, divided
Skins from 3 large brown onions
1 large red beet, peeled and chopped
¾ cup "cut and sifted" hibiscus flowers
¼ cup ground turmeric
Boiling water

—→

In another saucepan, combine the onion peels, 3 cups water, 1 tablespoon vinegar, and 4 eggs. (For a cool tie-dye effect, you can wrap the eggs in the onion peels and secure the peels with rubber bands.) Simmer for 30 minutes, then refrigerate overnight. (Yes, these eggs will be over-cooked, but the deep brick color is worth it.)

Finally, in each of three small pans, medium mixing bowls, or large glass jars, add the beet, hibiscus, and turmeric separately. (Avoid using plastic since the dyes will color it.) Add 3 cups boiling water and 1 tablespoon vinegar to each vessel and stir to combine. Gently submerge 4 or more eggs into each vessel, adding up to 1 cup more boiling water to the hibiscus if the liquid doesn't quite cover the eggs (the flowers will absorb some liquid). Add any remaining eggs to the dye of your choice.

Leave all the eggs to soak overnight in the fridge, or for best results, a full 24 hours. Gently pat the eggs dry with paper towels (the hibiscus eggs will need a rinse with cool water), then hide, eat, use for Easter Egg Breads (page 115), or refrigerate for up to 1 week.

A PAVLOVA IS A BAKED MERINGUE DESSERT—a fairly simple thing of beauty, made by whipping up egg whites and sugar, stirring in a few other ingredients, and baking in a super-low-temperature oven until each pavlova is shattery and shiny on the outside but marshmallow-soft on the inside. Growing up, I'd often make meringue cookies with my mom, which are very similar, but making pavlovas takes it up a notch. I fill them with whipped cream and whatever berries look best at the market or off our summer berry plants. If you're feeling celebratory, spike the berry mixture with ¼ cup Grand Marnier or Cointreau—it adds a lovely orange flavor with only a light bite.

Don't get too serious when you're forming the pavlovas; their rusticity is part of their charm. This is always a fun one to have little hands help with too!

STRAWBERRY PAVLOVAS

Makes 8 pavlovas

Preheat the oven to 300 degrees F. Line a rimmed baking sheet with parchment paper and set aside.

To make the pavlovas, in the bowl of a stand mixer fitted with the whisk attachment, whip the egg whites on high speed until soft peaks form, about 1 minute. Reduce the speed to low and slowly add the sugar, then return to high speed and whip for about 4 minutes, or until the whites are thick and glossy and when you rub a bit of the mixture between two fingers, you don't feel any granules. (Alternatively, you can use a hand mixer, but it will take a minute or two longer—and it will feel like forever.) Add the cornstarch, vanilla, and vinegar, and mix again on medium speed for about 30 seconds, stopping to scrape down the sides of the bowl halfway through.

Use a fingertip-size dab of the meringue to "glue down" each of the four corners of the parchment. (This helps prevent the sheet from moving too much as you spread the meringue.) Using 1 scant cup for each pavlova, drop 8 large dollops of meringue onto the baking sheet, spacing them evenly. Using the back of a spoon, make a well in the center of each pavlova, pressing about halfway down into the meringue and moving the spoon in a circle to create a divot that would fit an imaginary lemon half. Be sure to keep about an inch of space between pavlovas because they will expand slightly.

FOR THE PAVLOVAS
6 large egg whites, at room temperature
1⅓ cups sugar
1 teaspoon cornstarch
1 teaspoon vanilla extract
1 teaspoon distilled white vinegar

FOR THE TOPPINGS
2 quarts strawberries, hulled, halved, and sliced crosswise
¼ cup plus 2 tablespoons sugar, divided
¼ cup orange-flavored liqueur, such as Grand Marnier or Cointreau (optional)
Pinch of kosher salt
2 cups heavy cream

■—→

Reduce the oven temperature to 200 degrees F and bake for 3 hours, rotating the pan halfway through, or until you see small cracks begin to form on the sides of each pavlova. Without opening the oven door, turn off the oven and let the pavlovas cook for 1 more hour as the oven cools. Remove from the oven and let cool to room temperature. (The pavlovas will look about the same as they did when they went in. If some of them have merged, gently break them apart.)

While the pavlovas cool, make the toppings. In a medium bowl, mix the strawberries with ¼ cup of the sugar, the liqueur, and salt and set aside for the berries to get juicy.

In the bowl of a stand mixer fitted with the whisk attachment, whip the cream on medium-high speed until soft peaks form, about 2 minutes. Add the remaining 2 tablespoons sugar and whip again on medium speed until medium-firm, another 30 seconds or so.

To serve the pavlovas, fill them with whipped cream and top with as many berries as they will hold, maybe spilling some down the side too. Pass any extra berries at the table. To make ahead, wrap completely cooled pavlovas well in plastic and store for up to 24 hours. You can also refrigerate the cream and strawberries, covered, up to 24 hours as well.

DOWN-HOME RANCH DINNER

Menu for 10 to 12

ON A RANCH IN FAR NORTHERN CALIFORNIA'S SCOTT VALLEY, the definition of "home" has become much broader for us. We spend much of our time working with our animals, and our land is our home most days. Every day is guided by the weather and by the chores the day brings, so what happens outside is just as important—if not more so—than what happens inside.

Early in the spring, taking care of our home means shearing all our sheep (except the lambs, whose wool hasn't grown enough to make them too hot in the summers). Because sheep-shearing takes years to perfect, we hire skilled shearers to remove each animal's wool quickly and in one piece. It's a big event for a few days, and we usually bring in the neighbor boys to have extra hands; after two full days of shearing, we wind up with upwards of 4,000 pounds of wool, which we use during the winter to insulate the pigs' huts and the cows' watering troughs on the hill.

After a hard day of work on the ranch, it's nice to come home to hearty food cooked low and slow. We'll often make a double batch of chili—enough to share with everyone who's helped throughout the day—and maybe a sweet treat to enjoy together afterward in front of a crackling fire when the work is done.

MENU TIPS

It's best to make the cornbread right before serving, but you can prepare the Caesar dressing and the cake batter up to 3 days ahead, then just pop the cakes in the oven whenever you're ready for dessert. Same for the chili: you can serve it immediately or make it up to 3 days ahead, let it mellow in the fridge, and reheat it when you're ready.

I LOVE A LITTLE CRUNCH in my Caesar salad, but it doesn't have to come from a crouton. For great salty, flavorful bursts, I turn Pecorino cheese into toasty little chips to sprinkle all over the greens. Combined with an easy blender Caesar dressing, you've got this twist on a classic salad that will become a house favorite.

On its own, this salad makes a great lunch or dinner for four with Grilled Bread (see page 184) and a little leftover grilled steak or chicken on top, but it serves twelve easily as a side with a hearty bowl of chili.

CAESAR SALAD <u>WITH</u> PECORINO CRISPS

Makes 10 to 12 side servings or 4 dinner servings, plus 1¼ cups dressing

First, make the dressing. In the work bowl of a food processor or blender, process the olive oil, lemon juice, cream, anchovies, garlic, egg yolk, Dijon, Worcestershire, salt, pepper, and cayenne until well blended. Add 1 ounce (½ cup) of the Pecorino and pulse to incorporate, then transfer the dressing to a mason jar or serving bowl. Set aside or refrigerate, covered, for up to 3 days. (If you're going to make the dressing in advance, skip the egg yolk.)

To make the Pecorino crisps, heat a 9- or 10-inch nonstick skillet over medium heat. Scatter 1 ounce (½ cup) of the cheese in as even a layer as possible over the bottom of the pan. Let the cheese melt and begin to bubble without disturbing it. When the cheese begins to turn brown and smoke a little, after about 2 minutes, remove the pan from the heat and set aside to cool for 3 minutes, or until when you use a rubber spatula to nudge the cheese, it breaks into shards. (It will darken as it sits.) Using the spatula, break the cheese into assorted-size crisps and transfer them to a plate. Wipe out the pan and return it to the heat. Repeat with the remaining 1 ounce cheese. (If you can catch the cheese at just the right moment—when it's still slightly pliable but firm enough to hold together—you can actually move the entire crisp to a plate at once, and it cools into one giant cracker.) The crisps can also be made up to 3 days ahead and stored in an airtight container at room temperature.

To serve, in a large mixing bowl, toss the romaine with dressing to taste, taking care to coat all the leaves. Transfer the salad to a serving platter, season with more pepper, and top with Pecorino crisps.

½ cup extra-virgin olive oil

⅓ cup freshly squeezed Meyer lemon or regular lemon juice (from 2 or 3 large lemons)

¼ cup heavy cream

5 jarred anchovies

3 large cloves garlic

1 large egg yolk (optional)

2 teaspoons Dijon mustard

2 teaspoons Worcestershire sauce

1 teaspoon kosher salt

½ teaspoon freshly ground black pepper

Pinch of cayenne (optional)

3 ounces (1½ packed cups) finely grated Pecorino-Romano cheese, divided

1 large head romaine lettuce or 4 trimmed bagged romaine hearts (about 1 pound total), cut into bite-size pieces (about 10 packed cups)

THIS IS THE ULTIMATE MEAT-LOVER'S CHILI. It's also a great way to cook brisket! Made with slow-cooked chunks of brisket that become tender with a few hours' cooking time, plus the traditional ground beef, it has a gentle background heat as well as a natural sweetness from the sweet potatoes. What I love best about chili is that it's infinitely flexible and expands to feed whoever needs to be fed. And of course, this one also freezes well.

DOUBLE-BEEF CHILI <u>WITH</u> BLACK BEANS AND SWEET POTATOES

Makes 8 to 10 servings

First, brown the meat. In a large Dutch oven over medium-high heat, heat 2 tablespoons of the oil until shimmering. Add the ground beef, break it up with a spoon, and season with salt and pepper. Cook, stirring and breaking up the meat occasionally, until cooked through and beginning to brown, about 10 minutes. Using a slotted spoon, transfer the beef to a large bowl.

Add the remaining 2 tablespoons oil to the pan. Season the brisket chunks on all sides with salt and pepper, add them to the pan, and cook until browned on all sides, turning only once the beef releases easily from the pan, 10 to 15 minutes total. Transfer the brisket to the bowl with the ground beef, leaving enough fat in the pan to coat the onions (about 2 tablespoons).

Reduce the heat to medium and if the pan seems dry, drizzle in a little more oil. Add the onions, season with salt and pepper, then cook and stir until soft, about 5 minutes. Add the chili powder, cumin, coriander, garlic powder, and oregano, and cook, stirring constantly, for 2 minutes, or until the spices are fragrant and beginning to stick to the pan. Add the water, stirring and scraping the bottom of the pan as it bubbles away for a minute or two, then add the crushed tomatoes and tomato sauce and stir to combine.

Allow the mixture to come to a simmer, then stir in the beans with their liquid, chilies, sweet potatoes, and all the reserved beef. Return to a simmer, then reduce the heat to the lowest setting, cover, and cook the chili for 3 hours, stirring every hour or so.

Season to taste with additional salt and chili powder then serve piping hot, garnished with shredded cheese, sour cream, sliced jalapeños, and chopped onions. Allow any leftover chili to cool completely before storing in the fridge, covered, for up to 3 days. Reheat over low heat, stirring occasionally, for about 15 minutes before serving.

4 tablespoons neutral cooking oil, plus more as needed, divided
2 pounds ground beef
Kosher salt and coarsely ground black pepper
2 pounds beef brisket, thick fat trimmed, cut into 1-inch pieces
2 medium yellow onions, chopped
2 tablespoons ancho chili powder, plus more as needed
2 teaspoons ground cumin
2 teaspoons ground coriander
1 teaspoon garlic powder
1 teaspoon dried oregano
2 cups water
1 (28-ounce) can crushed tomatoes
1 (15-ounce) can tomato sauce
3 (15-ounce) cans low-sodium black beans
1 (4-ounce) can diced green chilies
1 pound sweet potatoes, cut into ¾-inch pieces
Shredded Monterey Jack or cheddar cheese, sour cream, sliced jalapeños, and chopped onions, for serving (optional)

10 THINGS TO DO WITH GROUND BEEF

Ground beef is one of the most popular items we sell. Since half the meat we get from any steer will always be ground, there is a lot of it! But our ground beef really stands apart from store-bought ground beef. And it's no wonder: our all-natural beef is dry-aged for 21 days for incomparable flavor. Frequently, customers purchase ground beef in our 10-pound or 20-pound family packs. While some larger families go through it quickly, others just use it a pound at a time. People are always, always looking for new ideas for ground beef! Here are ten go-tos that our family loves.

1. **BEEF TAQUITOS:** Stir together **1 pound of beef** with **1½ teaspoons kosher salt** and **½ teaspoon each black pepper**, **chili powder**, **cumin**, **onion powder**, and **garlic powder**. Stir in **8 ounces (2 cups) shredded cheddar** or **Monterey Jack cheese**, and roll the mixture into pan-warmed **6-inch corn tortillas**. Brush the tortillas with oil and bake in a 400-degree-F oven for about 20 minutes, flipping halfway through, or until browned and crisp. *(Makes 24 taquitos.)*

2. **MEATBALL SUBS:** Make the meat mixture from **One-Pan Spicy Meatball Bake (page 18)**, then roll it into 12 meatballs and bake on a parchment-lined baking sheet for about 20 minutes at 400 degrees F, or until browned. Drain on paper towels, then load into **4 (6-inch) sandwich rolls**, drizzle with **store-bought spaghetti sauce**, top with **slices of mozzarella**, and broil until the cheese is melted and bubbling. *(Makes 4 servings.)*

3. **QUICK JALAPEÑO POPPERS:** Cook **1 pound of beef** over medium heat until evenly browned, drain, and cool, then stir in **8 ounces softened cream cheese**, **2 cups shredded pepper jack cheese**, **1½ teaspoons chili powder** or **taco seasoning**, and **salt and pepper** to taste. Load the mixture into **12 large halved and scraped jalapeños** (about **1½ pounds whole jalapeños**), then bake at 450 degrees F until golden brown, about 15 minutes. *(Makes about 2 dozen.)*

4. **QUICK KOREAN-STYLE BEEF BOWLS:** Cook **1 pound of beef** over medium heat in **1 tablespoon vegetable oil** until evenly browned, then add **2 finely chopped cloves garlic** and **1 tablespoon chopped fresh ginger**, and stir for a minute or so, until fragrant. Add **2 tablespoons soy sauce**, **1 tablespoon mirin or rice vinegar**, and **2 teaspoons toasted sesame oil**, and stir until the liquid reduces and glazes the beef, then serve with **short-grain white rice, steamed broccoli or bok choy, sliced green onions**, and **kimchi**. *(Makes 3 to 4 servings.)*

5. **QUICKER BEEF POTPIE:** Follow the filling recipe for **Lamb and Root Vegetable Potpie with Leaf Lard Biscuit Crust (page 35)**, using **beef** instead of the lamb. While it's still warm, pile the filling into a 9-by-13-inch baking dish, then trim **a sheet of fridge-thawed puff pastry** to fit into the pan. Brush the crust with **beaten egg** and bake at 425 degrees F until the top is puffed and golden brown, about 20 minutes. *(Makes 6 to 8 servings.)*

6. **BRIAN'S FAVORITE BREAKFAST BURRITO:** Make the **beef for taquitos** (idea #1), then pile about ½ cup of it into each of **6 warmed 10-inch flour tortillas**. Top with **leftover cooked potatoes** and **6 scrambled eggs**. Serve rolled up with **salsa**, **guacamole**, and **sour cream**. *(Makes 6 servings.)*

7. **BEEF KOFTA PATTIES:** Mix **1 pound of beef** with **¼ cup finely minced red onion, 3 finely chopped cloves garlic, 2 teaspoons dried oregano, 1 teaspoon each ground cumin, ground coriander,** and **salt,** and **plenty of black pepper.** Form the beef into about 12 (2-inch) patties and cook in a skillet in **¼ inch of olive oil** over medium-high heat until well browned and cooked through, then drain and stuff into **warmed pita bread** with **thinly sliced cucumbers, tomatoes, red onion,** and **lettuce.** Serve with **plain yogurt seasoned with garlic and lemon juice.** *(Makes 4 servings.)*

8. **EASY SLOPPY JOES:** Mix **1 pound of cooked beef** with **1 cup spaghetti sauce** and **1 cup barbecue sauce** in a medium saucepan; simmer and stir over low heat for about 15 minutes, then pile into **4 burger buns.** *(Makes 4 servings.)*

9. **VIETNAMESE LEMONGRASS MEATBALLS:** Mix **1 pound of beef** with **2 tablespoons soy sauce, 2 tablespoons grated lemongrass, 1 tablespoon grated ginger, 1 tablespoon fish sauce, 1 tablespoon lime juice, 2 teaspoons grated fresh garlic, 2 teaspoons chili-garlic sauce,** and **plenty of salt and pepper.** Form into 1-inch meatballs, then cook in an oiled skillet over medium-high heat, turning occasionally, until well browned and cooked through, 10 to 12 minutes. Serve with **rice noodles** topped with **grated carrots** and **cucumbers** and **store-bought peanut sauce.** *(Makes 4 servings.)*

10. **A "WALKING TACO" FOR A QUICK LUNCH (LEGIT RODEO FARE!):** Open **a large snack-size bag of corn chips** or **nacho-flavored tortilla chips** lengthwise and pile on about **½ cup warmed leftover taco meat** (or the taquito meat from idea #1), **shredded lettuce, cheese, sour cream,** and **pico de gallo** or **salsa.** *(Makes 1 serving.)*

I LOVE TO COOK SAVORY, MEATY RECIPES most days; the precision and perfection involved in a lot of baking projects isn't my strong suit, and my girls are the same way. We prefer baked goods that are adaptable—things that won't fail catastrophically if we don't measure perfectly, or will react well when we decide to add more or less chocolate. (Francie is famous for always adding more! See the Ranch-Size Kitchen-Sink Cookies on page 25.)

But I do want the girls to be confident bakers, which is why I encouraged them to start with cornbread since it has a very flexible personality. These muffins are no exception: while they are slightly more tender if you fold in the flour at the last moment, they're still nearly perfect if you dump every single ingredient into a bowl and just stir it up before loading the batter into the pan. That means they're great for kids—even Tessa, our youngest, can do everything herself. She might even lecture her older sisters on making sure there are no lumps in the baking powder.

Twelve muffins don't stand a chance of making it to breakfast the next day in our house, but if you have leftovers, split them top to bottom and reheat them cut side down in a buttered cast-iron skillet for breakfast. And if you want to cook the cornbread in big servings like we do at the Burgerhouse, substitute six 1-cup aluminum foil pie pans or ramekins for the muffin tin.

TESSA'S DUMP-AND-STIR CORNBREAD MUFFINS

Makes 12 muffins or 6 mini loaves

Preheat the oven to 400 degrees F. Generously butter a 12-cup muffin pan (or six 1-cup aluminum foil pie pans or ceramic ramekins) and set aside.

In a large mixing bowl, use a wooden spoon to gently stir together the eggs, cornmeal, cream, melted butter, sugar, baking powder, and salt until all the ingredients are moistened, then fold in the flour and mix until smooth.

Divide the batter evenly between the greased muffin cups, piling a heaping ⅓ cup into each (or ⅔ cup each for foil pans or ramekins). The muffins cups will be quite full. Bake on the middle rack for about 15 minutes (17 minutes for mini loaves), or until domed, cracked, and golden brown on top. Slide a knife around each muffin immediately and carefully transfer to a wire rack. Serve piping hot or at room temperature. Store in an airtight container at room temperature for up to 1 day, and reheat in a 300-degree oven for 5 minutes before serving.

5 large eggs
2 cups fine-grind cornmeal
1 cup heavy cream or milk
½ cup (1 stick) unsalted butter, melted and cooled slightly, plus more for greasing the pan
⅓ cup sugar
1 tablespoon baking powder
2 teaspoons kosher salt
1½ cups all-purpose flour

THESE LITTLE CHOCOLATE CAKES ARE GREAT as an after-dinner treat when we have guests over. The chipotle chili powder gives them a spicy edge (which is optional but really what makes me and Brian love them). You can make and bake them all at once, or make and refrigerate them until just before you want to bake them. Or just serve half of them the day of and freeze the rest so that when no one's looking, you can bake one off for yourself (or your kids) on those nights when dessert is a necessity. Note that you're looking for the really tiny mason jars—the ½-cup/4-ounce size.

FLOURLESS CHIPOTLE CHOCOLATE POP-UP CAKES

Makes 12 cakes

Preheat the oven to 375 degrees F. Grease 12 (4-ounce/½-cup) mason jars or ramekins with butter and arrange them on a rimmed baking sheet.

In a double boiler set over medium-low heat (or a medium metal mixing bowl set over a saucepan with about 1 inch of simmering water), melt the butter and chocolate, stirring frequently, until completely smooth. Remove the boiler pan or bowl from the heat, add both sugars and the chili powder, and whisk until combined. Whisk in the eggs one at a time, until each one is completely incorporated.

Divide the batter among the prepared jars, adding about 6 table-spoons to each.

Transfer the baking sheet to the middle rack of the oven and bake for 15 to 17 minutes, or until the cakes have puffed and popped up above the edges of the jars but are still a bit glossy in the center. (Glossy centers mean the cakes are still a bit gooey; cook the cakes a little longer if you want them fully firm.)

The cakes are ready to serve piping hot, but you can also wait and serve them at room temperature if you prefer. Serve with the cream so each person can drizzle a teaspoon or two into the center of the cake before eating.

NOTE: You can prepare the batter, transfer it into the jars, cover them, and then refrigerate for up to 3 days before baking (uncovered) directly from the fridge for 18 to 21 minutes. You can also freeze them, covered, for up to 2 weeks. If you're baking the cakes from frozen, let them thaw at room temperature for about 5 minutes, then remove the lids and bake for 24 to 26 minutes.

1 cup (2 sticks) unsalted butter, cubed, plus more for greasing the jars

8 ounces bittersweet chocolate, chopped

1 cup granulated sugar

½ cup packed dark brown sugar

½ teaspoon chipotle chili powder (optional)

6 large eggs

½ cup heavy cream (optional)

FIESTA FRIDAY

Menu for 12

DURING A TYPICAL WEEK ON THE RANCH, we have help from a great team. In the Five Marys Farm Store, which we use as our home base for shipping our meat boxes, we have a small staff we refer to as "the shop gals." Brian has some help on the ranch too, mostly from our high school–age neighbor boys (who are about as capable as any adult men we've ever hired).

In the shop, the gals and I ship out hundreds of boxes packed with dry ice each week, all containing meat for our farm club members (who get big, personalized boxes monthly or quarterly) and for individual orders that come in throughout the course of the week. Most Mondays, Tuesdays, and Wednesdays, the team and I are in the shop as early as 5 or 6 a.m., printing shipping labels and making sure our assembly line of boxes, dry ice, packing material, and tape are ready. At 8 a.m. we stop quickly for a breakfast burrito at the café across the street. Then it's all hands on deck. We spend about five hours filling an entire UPS truck—or during the holidays, two or three— with upwards of 6,000 pounds of meat, and it goes out immediately for overnight delivery. Then we treat our staff to a well-earned lunch at the Burgerhouse, because each day we ship feels like running a marathon. It is the epitome of teamwork. Wednesday nights are our staff's fun "Friday" nights since we are done shipping for the week—we often meet at the bar for whiskeys, or cook dinner for everyone up at Camp.

Each Thursday and Friday, we catch up and get ready for the next week, restocking our shop freezers as more meat returns from our butchery and getting ready for the next week's wave. But reliably there's some sort of emergency or larger-scale ranch chore—say, working cattle for the day in the corrals, or spending an afternoon making our M5 Spice Rub (see page 21)—and our staff really deserve a celebratory meal. Then we call for a Fiesta Friday, complete with excellent cocktails, a full taco bar, and all the fixings. It's the best way we know how to thank our team for all they do.

MENU TIPS

Tacos are misleading in that the amount of meat you make tends to serve far more people than you might think. If you make just one of the taco recipes (either carnitas or beef tongue), you'll have enough meat for about 12 tacos, which will serve about 6 people having 2 each, with a bit of leftover meat. The two together will serve 8 or more, but if you make the entire menu and expect each person to have 2 tacos plus a bunch of sides, it will stretch to serve 12. Note that if you want to work ahead, you can make both the carnitas and the beef tongue a day (or three) before you plan to serve them, then simply broil them (on the same pan) right before you eat.

MY COCKTAIL MUSE IS BRIAN'S SISTER, KATHERINE. She's inspiring in every way, actually; I was very lucky to find a sister-in-law who is a best friend and gives me so many great recipe ideas! When we get together—never without a cocktail—Kat makes the best margaritas with just the right amount of sweetness.

But I also love palomas, which are cocktails traditionally made with tequila, a squeeze of lime, and either grapefruit juice and soda or Mexican grapefruit soda. This cocktail is a Kat-approved mix of the two drinks, blushed pink with a syrup made from tart hibiscus tea and honey. For spice, I add a bit of ground chili to the salted rim. If you want a sparkly drink on the lighter side, fill about a third of the glass with soda water before you add the palomita mixture.

HIBISCUS PALOMITAS

Makes 8 cocktails

Put the tea bags or dried hibiscus in a medium bowl and add the boiling water and honey. Let sit for 20 minutes, then remove the tea bags (or strain out the flowers) and refrigerate until fully chilled, about 2 hours.

In a gallon-size pitcher, large bowl, or in two 1-quart mason jars, stir together 1 cup of the hibiscus mixture with the tequila, citrus juices, and Cointreau. Taste the mixture: if you want it a little sweeter, you can add in the remaining hibiscus syrup to taste. To serve immediately, pour about 1½ cups over ice in a cocktail shaker and shake to chill. Pour the kosher salt onto a small plate and stir in the Aleppo pepper. Rub the rims of two 12-ounce (or similar) cocktail glasses with one of the lime slices, then invert each glass and dip it into the salt to coat the rims. Fill each glass with ice, add a lime slice to each, and pour in the chilled palomita. Repeat with the remaining glasses and mixture.

To serve the palomitas later, simply chill the mixture, covered, overnight or for up to 3 days. Stir or shake to blend and then pour directly into prepared glasses—no need to shake it on ice once it's good and cold.

3 bags hibiscus tea, or ¼ cup "cut and sifted" dried hibiscus blossoms

1½ cups boiling water

¼ cup honey

2 cups good tequila

2 cups grapefruit juice (ideally freshly squeezed)

1 cup freshly squeezed lime juice (from about 10 medium limes)

¼ cup Cointreau or other orange-flavored liqueur

Large ice cubes or crushed ice, for serving

¼ cup kosher salt

1 tablespoon ground Aleppo pepper (optional)

8 rounds thinly sliced lime, for garnish

ONE OF OUR SHOP GALS, Amy, introduced the entire ranch team to putting pomegranate seeds in guacamole. We all loved it because the tartness of the pomegranate seeds contrasts so well with the creamy, rich avocado. Now Maisie, our resident guac expert, insists that it's the best way to make guacamole. Maisie sometimes scoops the avocado flesh out of the peels with her hands—she swears it makes it easier to mash later.

MAISIE'S GUACAMOLE

Makes 5 cups

In a medium bowl, mash together the avocado, lime juice, and salt. Season to taste with additional lime juice and salt, then gently fold in the pomegranate seeds. Serve immediately, or cover the surface directly with plastic wrap and refrigerate for up to 24 hours, then stir before serving.

8 medium ripe avocados

2 tablespoons freshly squeezed lime juice, plus more as needed

1½ teaspoons kosher salt, plus more as needed

1 cup pomegranate seeds (from 1 large pomegranate)

HERE'S THE VERSION OF TACOS I MAKE for feeding a crowd—carnitas with a little kick. While traditional carnitas are made by refrying pork on the stovetop after it's cooked, I crisp it in the broiler. It means there's less hands-on time, and all the pork comes out hot at the same time, which is great when there's a full house.

You can also make the carnitas in a multicooker if you prefer. Cut the pork into 2- to 3-inch pieces and use the sauté function for browning the pork before cooking on high pressure for 50 minutes and letting the pressure release naturally.

CAMP CARNITAS TACOS

Makes 6 servings, or 12 tacos

Preheat the oven to 325 degrees F.

Heat a large Dutch oven with a lid over medium-high heat. Pat the pork dry and season all over with the salt. When the pan is hot, add the canola oil, then the pork, and sear until well browned on all sides, turning occasionally only when the meat releases easily from the pan, about 15 minutes total.

When the meat is browned, transfer it to a plate. Add the onion to the pot, stir for a moment or two, then add the garlic, jalapeños, chili powder, cumin, coriander, paprika, and black pepper. Cook and stir for about a minute, until the spices coat the onions, then add the vinegar and cook for a minute more, stirring to scrape any brown bits off the bottom of the pan. Nestle the pork back into the onions, add the broth, and bring to a simmer.

Cover the pot and transfer it to the oven. Cook the pork for 2½ to 3 hours, turning halfway through. When the center of the meat can be pierced easily with a fork, remove it from the oven and let it rest, covered, for 30 minutes.

Transfer the pork to a rimmed baking sheet. When cool enough to handle, remove and discard any large pieces of fat and use your fingers or two forks to shred the meat. Drizzle it with about 1 cup of the cooking liquid. (The liquid is delicious. You won't need more for tacos, but you can save it and use it in place of stock in a soup if you'd like!) If you want to make the pork ahead, you can stop at this point and refrigerate for up to 3 days in a covered container.

Preheat the oven broiler and position an oven rack about 3 inches from the heating element. Just before serving, broil the pulled meat on the baking sheet for 5 to 7 minutes, turning the meat and rotating the pan a couple of times during cooking, until the carnitas are piping hot and crisp in spots. Shower with sea salt and serve with the tortillas and toppings.

3 to 3½ pounds boneless (or 4 to 4½ pounds bone-in) pork shoulder or Boston butt, any strings removed
1 tablespoon kosher salt
2 tablespoons canola oil
1 yellow onion, roughly chopped
1 head garlic, halved through its equator
2 jalapeños, halved lengthwise
2 teaspoons ancho chili powder
2 teaspoons ground cumin
1 teaspoon ground coriander
1 teaspoon paprika
1 teaspoon freshly ground black pepper
⅓ cup apple cider vinegar
4 cups beef bone broth
Flaky sea salt
12 (6-inch) corn or flour tortillas, warmed
Toppings (see How We Do Tacos on page 151)

RANCHING GIVES US A DEEP APPRECIATION for the animals we raise—and nowhere is that more apparent than on our dinner plates. We eat or try to use as much as we can of every cut, because we know we've worked hard to raise animals whose fats are healthy and delicious. We are also keenly aware of waste, which means we teach our girls to eat the whole cow, quite literally.

It may sound exotic if you've never had it, but beef tongue is actually quite easy to cook. Like any large cut of meat, it benefits from long, slow cooking. But unlike most other cuts, it has an outer layer that needs to be removed. It's a pretty simple process: When the tongue is cooked, as soon as it's cool enough to handle, you can peel off the outer layer (which is a shade lighter in color) by hand or with the help of a small knife. Tongue is very tender and mild, so when you treat it like pork carnitas, giving it crispy edges right before serving, it's a great option for tacos.

CRISPY LENGUA TACOS

Makes 6 servings

In a large, deep pot or Dutch oven (with a lid) that's just big enough to hold the tongue, combine the tongue, broth, onion, garlic, thyme, bay leaves, chilies, salt, and peppercorns; season with ground black pepper; and bring to a simmer over medium-high heat. Cook the tongue, covered, for about 3 hours at a bare simmer, adjusting the heat as necessary and turning halfway through. When the center of the meat can be pierced easily with a fork or long skewer, transfer the tongue to a plate and set aside to cool.

When cool enough to handle, remove any large pieces of fat and use a small knife to trim, peel off, and discard the white outer layer of the tongue. Trim away any tough meat and fat at the base (thick end) of the tongue, then chop the remaining meat into ¾-inch cubes. Season the meat with salt and pepper, then transfer it to a bowl and drizzle with about ½ cup of the cooking juices. If you want to make the tongue ahead, you can stop at this point and refrigerate it for up to 3 days in a covered container.

Preheat the oven broiler. Transfer the meat to a rimmed baking sheet. Just before serving, broil it for 5 to 7 minutes, turning the meat and rotating the pan a couple of times during cooking, until piping hot and crisp in spots. Shower with sea salt and serve with the tortillas and toppings.

1 (3-pound) beef tongue, trimmed of excess fat
4 cups beef bone broth
1 yellow onion, halved
1 head garlic, halved through its equator
2 branches fresh thyme
3 bay leaves
3 dried ancho chilies
1 tablespoon kosher salt
1 tablespoon black peppercorns
¾ teaspoon black pepper
Flaky sea salt
12 (6-inch) corn or flour tortillas, warmed
Toppings (see How We Do Tacos on page 151)

TENDER, SMOKY BEANS WITH JUST A HINT OF SWEETNESS are the perfect sidekick to a taco party. But even on their own, they're a hit in our house. Brian loves having them around for burritos (and has been known to eat them cold, straight from the fridge) because they provide an instant burst of protein that gives him plenty of energy for working outside all day. With flavor from both our hickory-smoked bacon and naturally smoky mezcal, they also make a great base for a rice bowl—just add your favorite taco toppings and you've got an easy dinner.

We mail-order heirloom beans from California growers because we find they have better flavor and we like knowing they're grown well. They're more expensive than grocery store beans, but they're worth it.

For bacon-studded beans, you can chop the bacon before it goes into the pot, and leave it in for serving. If you prefer black beans, you can substitute them for the pinto beans.

SCRATCH SMOKY PINTO BEANS

Makes 8 to 12 servings

In a multicooker with a high-pressure setting, stir together the beans, broth, water, mezcal, onion, bacon, cinnamon sticks, and salt. Secure the lid and set to cook on high pressure for 1 hour. (Alternatively, you can cook the beans in a slow cooker on the high setting for 8 hours, stirring once or twice during cooking.)

Once done, allow the pressure to release naturally (about 20 minutes), then open the lid and test the beans. (If they aren't quite done, replace the lid and cook on high pressure for another 5 to 10 minutes, depending on doneness.) Stir in the sugar and let sit for a few minutes so it can dissolve. Season to taste with salt and pepper and remove the cinnamon sticks; you can choose whether to remove or serve the bacon and onion. Serve immediately or replace the lid and keep warm until ready to serve.

To store the beans, cool completely, transfer to an airtight container (with their liquid), and refrigerate up to 5 days. To reheat, transfer the beans and liquid to a small saucepan and reheat gently over low heat, stirring occasionally, until steaming.

1 pound dried pinto beans, rinsed and picked over
4 cups beef bone broth
1 cup water
½ cup mezcal, tequila, or freshly squeezed orange juice
1 medium yellow or white onion, halved
2 thick strips hickory- or applewood-smoked bacon, left whole or chopped
2 cinnamon sticks
1 tablespoon kosher salt
2 tablespoons demerara sugar or dark brown sugar
Freshly ground black pepper

TAJÍN IS A POWDERED CHILI-LIME SPICE that's highly versatile and delicious show-ered over everything from sliced mango to jicama to grilled corn. It's a great secret weapon for a spicy, tangy Mexican-inspired corn salad—one of Brian's favorites, because he loves anything spicy (the hotter the better). Using 1½ teaspoons here will give you a pleasantly piquant salad; if I'm making this just for our family, I split the salad in half and add more Tajín to the portion that Brian and I will share.

SPICY CORN SALAD

Makes 8 servings

In a large bowl, mix together the corn, tomatoes, onion, cilantro, lime juice, olive oil, peppers, and Tajín. Serve immediately, or chill, covered, for up to a day before serving.

Kernels from 8 cobs white or
    yellow corn (about 5 cups)
1 pint grape or cherry
    tomatoes, halved
¼ large red onion, thinly sliced
½ cup roughly chopped fresh
    cilantro (leaves and tender
    stems only)
¼ cup freshly squeezed lime
    juice (from 2 large limes)
¼ cup extra-virgin olive oil
2 serranos or small jalapeños,
    very thinly sliced
1½ teaspoons Tajín, plus more
    as needed

HOW WE DO TACOS

On the ranch, dinner is hard to plan with much precision; we never know if we'll have plenty of time to prepare a meal or if we'll all wind up coming in late after some unexpected chore crops up. One of my go-to solutions (besides teaching the girls to cook) has been to braise a pork shoulder in the corner of my test kitchen at least once a week. I'll slow-cook it in cider, or in a Dutch oven with orange juice and wedges, and it serves us for dinner and always leaves enough for the girls to use in quesadil-las or sandwiches when they're making themselves lunch (or elevenses or a 2 p.m. snack) at home. Their favorite version is pork carnitas because they all love tacos. We go all in on the toppings, which really take it up a notch. I like offering lots of options, including diced cherry tomatoes, sour cream, cubed avocado, shredded cabbage or lettuce, diced onion, chopped fresh cilantro, lime wedges, sliced radishes, salsa, pickled jalapeños, and Fermented Charred-Chili Hot Sauce (page 152) on the side.

DIY: FERMENTED CHARRED-CHILI HOT SAUCE

ANYONE WHO KNOWS ME AND BRIAN knows we love spicy food. Every summer, I make a huge batch of homemade hot sauce that usually lasts until the time the peppers get harvested late the next summer. From year to year the recipe changes—depending on whether I feel like charring the peppers (which adds depth and a lovely smoky flavor) and which chilies have done well in the garden that year. What doesn't change is that I leave the hot sauce on the counter in mason jars with very lightly sealed lids for a few days to let any good bacteria multiply naturally—a process I jump-start with naturally fermented fish sauce, which gives the finished hot sauce more flavor. This approach boosts taste but doesn't actually result in a fully fermented product, so the sauce does need to be either refrigerated or processed in a hot water bath to be shelf stable.

The sauce tastes best with just-picked peppers, but off-season hot sauce made with store-bought peppers is still more exciting than any old bottled sauce—and it makes for great gifts. So while I relish making it in the summer, I've been known to make batches for holiday or teachers' gifts, or whenever I am running low on my stash. Start with any combination of peppers you want as long as the total weight (just shy of 6 pounds) stays the same.

I like to leave the seeds in because I think they're pretty and I like the extra heat, but you can make the sauce without them if you prefer a slightly milder sauce.

Makes about 12 cups

Preheat the oven broiler on the highest setting. Position an oven rack about 4 inches from the top heating element.

Spread the jalapeños on a large baking sheet. Broil for 15 minutes, or until browned and blistered on all sides, turning occasionally. You want the peppers to take on some color, but you don't want them to get totally soft.

Transfer the jalapeños to a large bowl and put the poblanos, habaneros, serranos, onions, and garlic on the same baking sheet. Broil for about 15 minutes, again turning occasionally and rotating the pan, until the peppers are browned and blistered on all sides and charred in some spots and the onions are tinged with black. (If the garlic and small peppers become good and dark before the rest of the ingredients are done, you can pluck them off the pan first and allow the rest to continue cooking.)

4 pounds jalapeños, stemmed
1 pound poblanos or Anaheims, stemmed
8 ounces habaneros, stemmed
4 ounces serranos, stemmed
2 large yellow onions, cut into roughly 1-inch pieces
Cloves from 1 large head garlic (about 15 cloves), peeled
3 tablespoons fish sauce
3 tablespoons kosher salt
1½ cups apple cider vinegar

Set the pan aside and allow the peppers to cool (about 20 minutes), then pull out and discard the tops of every pepper and add the vegetables to the bowl with the jalapeños. Stir in the fish sauce and salt.

Puree the pepper mixture in a blender or food processor in batches until smooth, adding water as needed to make the sauce move in the blender. If you want a super thick sauce, add less water; add more for a thinner, more pourable mixture. (The consistency is up to you, but it's important that the sauce is uniform in color. I add about 3 cups of water total for this quantity of peppers, adding 1 cup to each of three batches in the blender, which produces a thick, spoonable sauce, almost more like a salsa.) Transfer the blended batches to another large bowl as you work.

Stir the combined batches to make sure the sauce is uniform, then cover with plastic wrap and let sit at room temperature for 24 to 72 hours, or until the sauce develops a pleasant smell and you begin to see small bubbles forming at the edges. (If you have a large glass container that fits all the sauce, use that so you can see whether any bubbles have formed on the sides. You can also ferment the sauce in mason jars, but you'll have to divide the vinegar evenly between each jar in the next step.)

Stir in the vinegar, season to taste, and transfer the sauce to a dozen 1-cup sterilized mason jars, leaving ½ inch of room at the top of each jar. Store the sauce in the refrigerator for up to 2 months as is, closing the container or lid loosely to allow air to escape, or process the jars for 20 minutes in a water bath per the manufacturer's instructions. Cool completely and store at room temperature in a dark place for up to 1 year.

NOTE: If you're not a fan of smoky flavors, or you're in a rush, you can skip the broiler and just slice up the fresh peppers and put them right in the blender.

CAMP OPENER COOKOUT

Menu for 6

WHEN BRIAN AND I BOUGHT THE RANCH, it had a two-bedroom 760-square-foot cabin (that was once a chicken coop) set right beside its much larger original eight-bedroom homestead house. We still live mostly in the Little House, as we call it, because it was easier to fix up than the Big House, but the one thing it has never been large enough to provide is a place for entertaining. For that, we built a covered outdoor kitchen and a big fire pit in an area that became known as Camp. At the time, we were still working really hard to build up our meat business customer base. We thought that if we had a place where people could visit, taste our meat, and experience our way of life, we'd earn lifelong customers. We built a butler's kitchen with a triple sink in the back (so there was a hidden place for doing dishes) and planned to host guests overnight in glamping tents we put up nearby.

Today, we use Camp (the kitchen, dining space, and tents) for friends and family and occasional events, opening it up each year around Memorial Day, when it's warm enough to sleep outside, and closing it in October, as soon as the pipes threaten to freeze. Each year, the first feast of the season—our summer opener—is usually the most memorable.

MENU TIPS

Start the ribs and mix the spiked tea the night before for best flavor. On the day you plan to serve them, put the ribs on the grill and putter about making everything else while they cook. (You'll have time to watch a sunset.) To stretch the menu to feed eight or ten, add Scratch Smoky Pinto Beans (page 149) or Tessa's Dump-and-Stir Cornbread Muffins (page 134)—or both!—to the menu.

I DON'T DRINK COFFEE, which surprises most people, but I do love a tall glass of iced tea when the weather warms. And if it comes with a little kick? Even better after the chores are done.

This is a great cocktail to sip while you are still enjoying the afternoon sun—a spiked version of an Arnold Palmer sweetened with honey and flavored with orange and lemon zest for a little more pop. It's light enough that you can have more than one, which makes it ideal for guests to sip all afternoon while I show them around the Camp kitchen and tend to a big batch of ribs on the grill.

Note that this version is just sweet enough. If you like a true Southern-style sweet tea, add 2 to 4 tablespoons of sugar to the mixture in addition to the honey. And of course, it will make a lovely iced tea without the vodka too. You can store the tea mixture, with vodka and citrus juices added, for up to a week in the fridge.

SWEET CITRUS SPIKED ICED TEA

Makes 6 cocktails

In a large pitcher or glass measuring cup, combine the boiling water and tea bags, and steep according to package instructions, about 4 minutes. Remove the tea bags and stir in the citrus zests and honey, stirring until the honey is fully dissolved. Cool to room temperature (about 1 hour), then remove the citrus zests and chill until cold, about 4 hours. Stir in the vodka and citrus juices.

To serve, fill six tall glasses with ice and pour a scant cup of the mixture into each glass. Garnish with citrus slices and serve.

4 cups boiling water
4 bags English Breakfast, Earl Grey, or similar tea
Zest strips and juice of 1 Valencia or Cara Cara orange
Zest strips and juice of 1 Meyer lemon
½ cup honey
1 cup vodka, chilled
Lemon or orange slices, for garnish

IN ANY KITCHEN—AT HOME OR AT CAMP—I don't usually fuss with toasting whole spices, but when I want what I'm making to be spice-forward without actually being spicy, spending five minutes on toasting can make a huge difference. Here's a good example of when it's worth the effort: these spareribs get their deep, rich flavor from a dry rub made with toasted cumin and coriander seeds, and a simple honey-sweetened barbecue sauce made with some of the same spices plus a good splash of white vinegar. The time it takes to babysit the spareribs as they cook provides a great excuse to sit by the fire (or grill) with a friend for a few hours.

Note that spareribs and baby back ribs aren't the same thing; spareribs come from a pig's belly, while baby back ribs come from the back (as the name suggests) and are usually much smaller and a little more tender. You can use spareribs, St. Louis–style ribs (which are basically trimmed spareribs), or baby back ribs for this recipe, just know that baby back racks will take less time to cook because of their smaller size and leaner meat.

CUMIN-CORIANDER SPARERIBS WITH HONEY BARBECUE SAUCE

Makes 6 servings

Heat a small dry skillet over medium heat. Add the cumin and coriander seeds and toast, shaking the pan occasionally, for about 2 minutes, or until the spices are fragrant and begin to pop. Transfer the seeds to a plate to cool, then coarsely grind in a mortar and pestle, spice grinder, or clean coffee grinder.

Place the ribs on a rimmed baking sheet and pat them dry with paper towels. In a small bowl, stir together the ground spices with the paprika, brown sugar, salt, and pepper until well blended. Set aside 3 tablespoons of the spice mixture for the sauce. Sprinkle the ribs on all sides with the remaining spice mixture, then use your hands to rub it into every little crevice. Set the ribs aside for 1 hour, or cover and refrigerate for up to 24 hours.

Prepare a hardwood fire for grilling, or heat a gas or charcoal grill to very low (250 to 275 degrees F). If the ribs were refrigerated, let them to come to room temperature as the grill heats.

When the grill is hot, brush the cooking grates clean. Add the ribs meaty side up and grill, covered, over indirect heat for 3 to 4 hours (2 to 3 hours for baby back ribs), turning and rotating the ribs every 30 minutes or so and keeping an eye on the grill temperature,

¼ cup whole cumin seeds

2 tablespoons whole coriander seeds

2 racks pork spareribs or 4 racks baby back ribs (about 6 pounds total), silver skin removed and excess fat trimmed

3 tablespoons hot or mild smoked Spanish paprika

2 packed tablespoons dark brown sugar

1 tablespoon plus 2 teaspoons kosher salt

1 teaspoon freshly ground black pepper

1 cup ketchup

½ cup honey

¼ cup distilled white vinegar

➤——

adding a few more pieces of charcoal or adjusting as needed. When the meat has pulled back from the ribs, exposing the bones, and the ribs threaten to tear apart when you pick them up with tongs because the meat is so tender, they're done.

While the meat cooks, make the sauce: In a small saucepan over medium heat, combine the reserved spice mixture, the ketchup, honey, and vinegar, and stir to combine. Bring to a simmer, then reduce the heat to low; cook for 5 minutes at a gentle bubble, stirring occasionally, and set aside off the heat until the ribs are done.

Brush the ribs liberally on both sides with the sauce and grill, covered, for another 5 minutes per side. Transfer the ribs to a platter and serve, passing any extra sauce at the table. (You can also cover and cool completely, then refrigerate for up to 48 hours; reheat the ribs for 15 minutes in a 300-degree oven before serving.)

COOKING SPARERIBS INDOORS

If you're not up for starting the grill—or you're craving spareribs when there's a blanket of snow outside—you can also cook ribs in the oven. Once the spice mixture has had a chance to flavor the meat, preheat the oven to 250 degrees F. Cover the ribs with aluminum foil and bake on the center rack, meaty side up, for 1 hour. (It's OK if the ribs overlap slightly.) Flip the ribs over, bone side up, and cook for another hour, then turn meaty side up again, remove the foil, and cook for another 30 to 90 minutes, depending on the size of your ribs, or until the meat pulls back from the bone tips. Remove the ribs from the oven, switch the heat setting to broil, and arrange an oven rack about 6 inches from the heating element. Brush the ribs on both sides with the barbecue sauce, then broil for 4 to 6 minutes, turning the ribs twice during cooking, or until the sauce is bubbling on top and has turned a shade darker. Transfer to a platter and serve with extra sauce alongside.

BACON, CUT FROM PORK BELLY, doesn't come in a neat rectangular slab on a hog. After bacon strips are trimmed and packaged in the tidy bundles you find on grocery store shelves, there are a lot of little leftover pieces, called bacon ends. On average, we get about a pound of bacon ends for every five pounds of strip bacon we package. Rather than let the ends go to waste, we package and sell them too.

They're the star of one of my favorite potato salads. After I crisp the bacon ends, I cook jalapeños and onions in the leftover fat, then pickle them with vinegar for a sharp tang that provides the perfect balance for the creaminess of the potatoes.

SALT-AND-VINEGAR POTATO SALAD WITH PICKLED JALAPEÑOS AND BACON ENDS

Makes 6 to 8 servings

In a small saucepan, bring about 3 inches of water to a boil over high heat. Carefully add the eggs, reduce the heat to a simmer, and cook for 11 minutes. Immediately transfer the eggs to a bowl of ice-cold water and set aside to cool.

Meanwhile, put the potatoes in a medium saucepan with enough water to cover. Bring to a boil over high heat, then reduce to a simmer and cook for 15 to 18 minutes, or until the largest pieces slide off a skewer or fork when pierced. Drain the potatoes and set aside until cool enough to handle.

Heat a large cast-iron skillet over medium heat, add the bacon, and cook, stirring occasionally, until crisp, about 10 minutes. Using a slotted spoon, transfer the bacon to a paper towel–lined plate, leaving the fat in the pan. Add the jalapeños and onion and cook, stirring occasionally, until softened and charred in spots, about 5 minutes. Transfer the vegetables to a large bowl, stir in the vinegar, salt, and pepper, and set aside to pickle for about 10 minutes.

Chop the eggs and slice the potatoes into ½-inch rounds (or half-moons). Add them to the bowl with the peppers and stir to combine, then stir in the bacon and set aside at room temperature for about an hour so the potatoes can soak up the vinegar.

Stir in the mayonnaise, sour cream, Dijon, and parsley; season to taste with salt and pepper, and serve immediately, or cover and refrigerate for up to 3 days.

4 large eggs

2½ pounds medium red potatoes (skins on), halved if large

½ pound smoked bacon ends or bacon strips, roughly chopped

2 large jalapeños, cut into ¼-inch-thick slices

½ medium red onion, halved again and cut into ¼-inch-thick slices

¾ cup distilled white vinegar

1 tablespoon kosher salt

¾ teaspoon freshly ground black pepper

½ cup mayonnaise

¼ cup sour cream

1 tablespoon Dijon mustard

2 tablespoons finely chopped fresh flat-leaf parsley leaves

EVERY SPRING, WE PLANT A GARDEN beside our house or up at Camp that becomes my favorite place as the weather warms up. It varies in size from year to year, growing as large as 25 by 50 feet and sometimes spilling over the edges. It's packed with a little of everything but always heavy on the tomatoes and various hot peppers. I also plant lots of basil and parsley (see page 169) for making chimichurri—one of our favorite steak or breakfast burrito toppings. Each morning, I walk through the rows to see how all the plants are doing, pinching off the tops of the herbs before they go to seed and harvesting whatever is ready. Reliably the first things to come up are peas, carrots, and radishes.

When I serve rich foods like ribs and potato salad, I enjoy having a light, tangy slaw alongside. This modern lemony version of traditional peas and carrots takes advantage of what grows just outside my door. Look to your own garden for variation; you could also make this with raw baby asparagus or zucchini in place of the peas.

EASY PEAS AND CARROTS SLAW

Makes 6 servings

In a medium mixing bowl, whisk together the lemon juice, olive oil, tahini, water, yogurt, sugar, and salt and pepper to taste. Stir in the herbs, then add the peas, radishes, and carrot. Stir to blend, adjust the seasoning as needed, and serve.

¼ cup freshly squeezed lemon juice (from 2 large lemons)
¼ cup extra-virgin olive oil
2 tablespoons well-stirred tahini
2 tablespoons water
2 tablespoons plain full-fat yogurt
1 teaspoon sugar
Kosher salt and freshly ground black pepper
¼ cup loosely packed chopped mixed fresh herbs (such as mint, parsley, chives, tarragon, dill, and/or basil)
1 pound snap peas, trimmed and thinly sliced lengthwise
4 radishes, trimmed and julienned
1 medium carrot, grated

ONE OF MY BEST FRIENDS growing up, Janna Mariani, has a cherry farm in Northern California, near Brentwood. They have a u-pick orchard with fresh sweet and sour cherries. My godson, James, helps manage the operation in the summers, and somehow his cherries taste better than anyone else's. There may be some bias involved, but I'm sure if you bake up this cherry galette—an extra-large and lemony version, made in a big cast-iron pan so it serves a crowd—it will be *almost* as good as the one I make using my favorite fruit from James.

SOUR CHERRY CAST-IRON GALETTE WITH LEMON AND THYME

Makes one 12-inch galette

Make the pie crust as directed. Working with a floured rolling pin on a lightly floured surface at least 20 inches square, roll the dough ball into an 18-inch round. (It will seem giant.) Drape the crust over a 12-inch cast-iron pan, gently pressing the dough into the corners as you go and allowing the excess dough to flop over the sides. Refrigerate for 20 minutes. (You can also cover and refrigerate for up to 24 hours; allow the dough to come back to room temperature until pliable before proceeding.)

Meanwhile, in a large mixing bowl, stir together the flour, sugar, lemon zest, thyme, and salt. Add the cherries and lemon juice and stir until all the cherries are well coated. Remove the crust from the fridge, dump in the filling and any loose bits, and pat the filling down flat. Fold the excess dough over the filling (the dough will overlap in places) and brush the top side of the dough with the egg wash, sneaking the brush between the dough layers to encourage them to adhere. Shower the crust and filling with sugar, then sprinkle with more chopped thyme and a few sprigs. Refrigerate for 1 hour.

Preheat the oven to 425 degrees F and position a rack in the center of the oven.

Bake the galette for 15 minutes. Without opening the oven, reduce the temperature to 375 degrees F and bake for another 70 to 80 minutes (less for fresh fruit, more for frozen), or until the crust is nicely browned and the filling is bubbling slowly. Let cool for at least 30 minutes, or completely, and serve.

1 recipe All-Purpose Double Pie Crust (recipe follows)
½ cup all-purpose flour
½ cup sugar, plus more for sprinkling
Zest and juice of 1 large lemon (about 1½ teaspoons zest plus 3 tablespoons juice)
1 tablespoon chopped fresh thyme leaves, plus more chopped leaves and sprigs for garnish
½ teaspoon kosher salt
2 pounds fresh or frozen pitted sour (pie) cherries
1 large egg beaten with 1 tablespoon water

➤——→

All-Purpose Double Pie Crust

Makes enough for one 9-inch double-crust pie

To make the crust, in the work bowl of a food processor, pulse the flour, sugar, and salt together to blend. Add the butter and pulse until the largest chunks of butter are about the size of peas. Transfer ¼ cup ice-cold water to a measuring cup with a spout, and stir in the vinegar. With the machine running, drizzle this mixture into the food processor. Once the initial liquid has been added, drizzle in another 2 to 4 tablespoons of ice water as needed, pulsing, until the crust is uniformly moist and begins to gather in the bottom of the work bowl. (The machine's tone will change.) Dump the dough into a mixing bowl and press into a ball. Use as directed, or separate into two mounds, press into 1½-inch discs, wrap well in plastic, and refrigerate 1 hour before using, or up to 3 days.

2¾ cups all-purpose flour

1 tablespoon sugar

1 teaspoon fine sea salt

1 cup plus 2 tablespoons (2¼ sticks) unsalted butter, cut into ½-inch cubes, chilled

½ cup ice-cold water, divided

1 tablespoon apple cider vinegar, chilled

NOTE: When using this crust for the galette (page 165), you're making a double-crust recipe for a single very large round of pastry. For the Cardamom Apple Pie with Hazelnuts (page 77), it's serving in a more traditional role of top and bottom crust. Regardless of how it will be used, it makes a great freezer staple. You can prepare the dough, pat it into two equal discs each about 1½ inches thick, wrap them well in plastic, and freeze for up to 3 months. To thaw, let the rounds sit overnight in the refrigerator, then set out at room temperature for about 30 minutes before rolling.

DIY: MOBILE HERB GARDEN

AROUND THE TIME WE START OPENING UP CAMP for the summer, we get serious about planting our garden. We always plant tons of peppers and tomatoes and squash, but the thing I use most frequently all summer long is the herb corner. One year, when the kids had outgrown their little red wagon, my mom was visiting and saw it was just sitting unused near the house. She had the great idea to drill holes in it and fill it with basil, parsley, and chives—and voilà, I had a mobile herb garden. You could also use a wagon as a temporary nursery for planting smaller herbs until they're big enough to fill their own pots on the porch.

If you want to start your garden on the early side, forgo the classic wagon and instead look for the kind that has wooden fencing about 8 inches above the wagon's rim. The fence is normally used to keep kids and gear inside, but you can use it as a makeshift greenhouse frame. Buy a roughly 3-by-4-foot section of clear plastic sheeting, lash a 2-foot stake or dowel to each end of the wagon, and drape the sheeting over the stakes and the wagon, securing it to the sides with twine or tape. Keep the cover on (except when you're watering) until the nights consistently stay at or above 50 degrees F.

And you probably don't need to be told, but I'll tell you anyway: if you plant mint, be cautious because it will take over the entire wagon. Since mint makes a great cocktail garnish, I still include it in my herb garden, but I make sure it stays in its own little pot so the roots don't run wild!

Makes a 10-plant mini herb garden

First, give the wagon some drainage. Using the drill, make 15 roughly evenly spaced holes in the bottom of the wagon, arranging them in 3 rows with the holes about 5 inches apart. Make sure some of the holes are in the deepest part of the wagon, between the ribs that line the bottom. Moisten a few paper towels and carefully wipe out any metal shavings.

Fill the wagon to the rim with dirt, then make 10 evenly spaced 4-inch-wide and 4-inch-deep hollows in the dirt. Remove the plants from their pots and gently loosen the roots, then snuggle them into the hollows and smooth the dirt around the perimeter, patting the dirt down over each root ball and adding additional dirt as necessary. When finished planting, water the garden, then add more dirt, as needed, to fill the wagon to just above the rim and water again.

Keep the wagon in a warm, sunny place at first, until the plants are established and the weather warms, then decide where it goes based on your area's climate and seasonal temperatures. Transfer large plants to other containers as they grow, and replace them with new smaller plants and fresh soil. And don't forget to water regularly!

1 used metal child's wagon (the more worn the better) with a seat area measuring roughly 33 inches long by 15 inches wide by 6 inches deep

1 cordless drill fitted with a ¼-inch metalworking or masonry bit

Paper towels

1½ cubic feet (about 40 liters) potting soil

10 (3-inch) herb plants (such as basil, thyme, oregano, rosemary, parsley, tarragon, sage, chives, cilantro, mint, or dill, or your favorite blend of herbs and lettuces)

Summer

OUR SUMMERS ARE SPENT OUTSIDE. Between irrigating, moving cattle between pastures, the girls practicing for rodeo, and entertaining the friends and family or guests we host at Camp, life happens under a great big California sky.

From a ranching perspective, summer means the animals are grazing on our green grasses, which means our job is largely about making sure their food is growing well by moving water and irrigation lines—sometimes twice a day. In June, when the ground is still somewhat wet, we water less frequently, but as summer progresses and the rains stop, managing how water gets used across the ranch and moving groups of cattle between smaller pastures as part of a rotational grazing system becomes Brian's biggest priority. We all pitch in to move wheel lines or fix the inevitable busted pipe, but it's really Brian who keeps our pastures (and hence our cattle) thriving.

The girls also compete in junior rodeos during the summer, giving us a chance to get off the ranch for a weekend and travel to another small town. We usually participate in a few rodeos across Northern California and Oregon—but there are also a lot of fun activities that don't even require leaving the ranch. All summer long, the girls sleep outside in bunks on the porch of the Little House or in tents in the front yard or in the bottle baby barn, and each night basically turns into a slumber party, complete with squealing and late-night stories (and the girls' kittens, who know a good sleeping buddy when they see one).

We sometimes hike up to the top of the property for a special campout, with dinner cooked over a fire, but even at home, we almost never eat inside. Once the outdoor kitchen is all set up at Camp, we cook our meals there most nights, or on the grill next to our roping arena. Every year, we also float the Scott River, which winds along the edge of our property, before grilling burgers back at Camp. Tessa's and Francie's birthdays are two days apart in mid-September, so our summers always end with a celebration.

MOUNTAIN-TOP CAMPOUT

Menu for 6

ON WARM SUMMER EVENINGS before fire season starts, we head up Sharp's Gulch—the historical name for the main draw on our property—past the cattle and horse pastures and way past the Camp kitchen, to a saddle between two mountains that offers views of our valley and one valley to the east. Atop the saddle, there's a vein of serpentine, California's state rock, so the girls call the spot Serpentine Saddle. Even when the weather is hot down on the ranch, the nights are cool up there. Brian helps the girls organize their gear, and they strategize about which way to make the trek up.

If you ask Tessa and Janie, they'll tell you that their favorite part of camping with their dad is getting to eat freeze-dried spaghetti—the kind that comes in a bag with instructions to just add boiling water. When they camp with Brian, they carry everything themselves backpacker-style, and they can eat what they want. But if I'm tagging along, I like to make it a little more about the food and bring some goodies to cook together over the fire. The girls hike or ride their horses up the mountain, and I drive up in an ATV with dinner supplies. We snack on trail mix while we set up camp and then start cooking something good and warming over the fire—a sausage stew, for example—because at 4,800 feet, the temperature drops as soon as the sun goes down. Maisie will usually wander off to collect some flowers or leafy greens to decorate whatever we're using as a table, Tessa might make a little rock garden, and Francie and Janie will work on their fire-building skills. After dinner, as the light fades, we grill peaches over the coals and top them with homemade ice cream.

It's always a fun mini adventure to make dinner or camp out on our land. What used to be a big undertaking—preparing for an entire weekend of camping at a spot we had to drive to—is now just a hike away in our own backyard. We never take that for granted!

MENU TIPS

This menu capitalizes on convenience so you're not transferring foods between pots and bowls when camping. Make the granola, trail mix, and ice cream base ahead, and if you can, cut up all the ingredients for the stew at home too—or don't, if you want something to do once you've set up camp!

WHEN WE STARTED OUR ONLINE M5 RANCH SCHOOL in 2020 as a way to bring cooking, crafts, and ranch-related skills and fun into kids' homes across the country, one of our first lessons was making homemade granola. It's a great way to get kids into the kitchen, as well as a convenient, portable go-to snack they can get by themselves any time of day.

I love the combination of coconut and dried cherries—and it's even better when the coconut comes in multiple forms. For my favorite granola, I use coconut oil and both flaked and chipped coconut for a variety of textures. Substitute other dried fruit—raisins, currants, or chopped dried apricots—for the cherries, if you prefer, and remember that granola is almost infinitely flexible. Make it your own!

RANCH SCHOOL COCONUT– CHERRY GRANOLA

Makes about 14 cups

Preheat the oven to 350 degrees F and position a rack in the center of the oven. Line a baking sheet with parchment paper and set aside.

In a large mixing bowl, stir together the oats, walnuts, coconut chips and flakes, almonds, salt, and cinnamon to combine. Add the oil, honey, and vanilla, and stir until everything is very well coated.

Transfer the mixture to the baking sheet and spread it into an even layer that goes all the way to the edges of the pan, patting it down well. Bake for 12 to 15 minutes, or until the edges just begin to brown, then stir the granola well and pat it down into an even layer again. Bake for another 15 minutes or so, or until well browned on top.

Allow the granola to cool completely, about 45 minutes. (If you don't like clumps, stir it occasionally as it cools.) Once cooled, break it up into pieces, stir in the cherries, and serve. The granola can be stored in an airtight container at room temperature for up to 2 weeks or frozen for up to 3 months.

5 cups (about 1 pound) old-fashioned rolled oats
1 cup whole or crushed walnuts
1 cup unsweetened coconut chips
1 cup unsweetened coconut flakes
⅔ cup sliced almonds
1 teaspoon fine sea salt
1 teaspoon ground cinnamon
⅔ cup coconut oil, melted
⅔ cup honey
1 teaspoon vanilla extract
1½ cups tart or sweet dried cherries

HAVING A PROTEIN-PACKED, SWEETS-SPIKED SNACK MIX on hand for hiking or camping is always convenient. Making trail mix from scratch, rather than purchasing it premixed, takes only a little bit more effort, and the results are always tastier.

When we take a group out on the trail or take the cousins camping, we start with a trail mix bar—a counter filled with bowls of all the bite-size nuts, seeds, dried fruit, and sweets you can possibly imagine. Give it a try and really go nuts (pun intended!): think beyond GORP (which stands for "good ol' raisins and peanuts") by combing the aisles of your local grocery store for tropical dried fruits, salty snacks like crunchy corn kernels or peanut butter-filled pretzels, and even sweets like gummies or jelly beans. Hand out lidded jars or ziplock bags and let everyone stuff them and shake them to mix everything together. I like to separate the ingredients into a few categories on the table and make sure the little ones have to pick a few "healthy" things, like nuts and fruit, before they get to pick a couple of the "treats," like chocolate or gummies. It usually makes for a much more balanced mix!

While the kids will dive right in to make some unusual concoction for their afternoon snack, adults are often a little hesitant. Here are a few adult-centric trail mix ideas that will keep you going all day long.

ALL-DAY TRAIL MIX

Makes about 2 cups (enough trail mix to fill a pint-size mason jar, plus a small handful for immediate snacking)

GOLDEN GORP MIX: ¾ cup dry-roasted peanuts, ½ cup golden raisins, ½ cup bittersweet chocolate chips, ¼ cup salted sunflower seeds

OREGON TRAIL MIX: 1 cup dry-roasted hazelnuts, ¼ cup dried cherries, ¼ cup dried apricots, ¼ cup pumpkin seeds, ¼ cup chocolate candies or chunks

CALIFORNIA FALL MIX (A.K.A. MARY'S FAVORITE TRAIL MIX): ½ cup roasted almonds, ½ cup prunes, ½ cup walnuts, ½ cup chocolate chips

OUR FIVE MARYS ITALIAN PORK SAUSAGE is so popular with our customers that it never fails to sell out quickly! Because of this, we don't usually get much for ourselves, so having it is a treat. I think it's best in soups and stews like this one, which really bring out the deep flavors of fennel and red pepper flakes.

I designed this stew with camping in mind—meaning there's no removing ingredients from a pan and setting them aside, and it's made with ingredients that are easy to transport (and prep ahead, if desired). Also, don't forget you can freeze the stock and use it as an ice block in your cooler if a drive is part of your adventure. It's fine if it's still partially frozen when you add it to the pot; simply start the simmering time once it comes to a boil.

OUR FAVORITE SAUSAGE STEW <u>WITH</u> GRILLED BREAD

Makes 6 servings

In a large Dutch oven with a lid over a medium (roughly 400-degree-F) hardwood fire with good coals (or on the stovetop over medium heat), melt the bacon fat. When fragrant, add the sausage and cook for about 10 minutes, or until browned all over, turning occasionally (and breaking it up, if using bulk sausage) when it releases easily from the pan. Add the onion, carrots, celery, and garlic; season with the thyme, red pepper flakes, salt, and pepper; and cook for 5 minutes or so, until the vegetables begin to take on a little color.

Add the tomato paste and cook, stirring, for a minute or two, until the paste coats all the ingredients at the bottom of the pan and begins to darken. Add the wine, stirring to scrape any browned bits off the bottom of the pan, then add the broth, potatoes, and kale, and season again with more salt and pepper.

Bring the liquid to a gentle simmer, cover, and cook for about 20 minutes, or until the potatoes and carrots are completely tender. (You may need to move the pot around if you're cooking over a live fire—to a hotter area if it's not quite simmering, or to a cooler one if it's boiling rapidly.) Taste and adjust the seasonings, then serve piping hot with the grilled bread or in bread bowls.

2 tablespoons bacon fat, olive oil, or butter

1 pound bulk Italian sausage, or 1½ pounds Italian sausage links, cut into 1-inch pieces

1 medium yellow onion, chopped

4 carrots (about ¾ pound), cut into ½-inch rounds

3 celery stalks, cut into ½-inch pieces

2 cloves garlic, crushed

¼ teaspoon dried thyme, or 1 teaspoon chopped fresh thyme leaves

Pinch of red pepper flakes

Kosher salt and freshly ground black pepper

2 tablespoons tomato paste

1 cup dry red wine

4 cups beef bone broth

1 pound red potatoes, cut into ½-inch pieces

2 packed cups chopped kale (from about ½ bunch), ribs included

6 (1-inch) slices of Grilled Bread (see page 184), or 6 (6-inch) sourdough boules, emptied to make bread bowls

GRILLED BREAD

I love having a hearty slice of bread to dip into soup, and it's hard to beat the toasty, smoky flavor of bread when it's grilled over a live fire. To grill bread, prepare a hardwood fire for grilling, or heat a gas or charcoal grill to medium (about 400 degrees F), and brush the cooking grates clean. Slice good sourdough bread into 1-inch slabs. Brush the slices generously on both sides with olive oil, then put the bread on the grill and toast until well browned on all sides, 6 to 8 minutes total, turning frequently. Over a live fire, you can also thread the bread onto s'mores skewers and roast, turning frequently, as you would a marshmallow, until golden brown all over.

NOTHING SIGNIFIES SUMMER ON THE RANCH like grilled peaches. There's a u-pick orchard on the other side of our mountain where we can stock up on juicy peaches when the season hits. We love to have them for dessert multiple times a week, simply cutting them in half to grill facedown on the barbecue and topping them with heavy cream or ice cream. To step it up, we make the ice cream ourselves, sweetening it partly with brown sugar for a more complex flavor. Top with an almond streusel made with jagged bread crumbs—from the same loaf you use for Our Favorite Sausage Stew with Grilled Bread (page 182)—for a unique crunch. And of course, for adults, it doesn't hurt to splash the peaches with bourbon when you turn them, if that's your style—I know it's mine!

CAMPFIRE PEACHES WITH SOURDOUGH STREUSEL AND BROWN SUGAR– VANILLA ICE CREAM

Makes 6 servings

Prepare a hardwood fire for grilling, or heat a gas or charcoal grill to medium (about 400 degrees F). Lightly brush the peaches on all sides with the canola oil and set aside.

In a small skillet over low heat (or on the side of the fire), melt the butter. When melted, increase heat to medium (or move the pan to the center of the fire), add the bread crumbs and almonds, and cook, stirring, until toasted and foaming, 3 to 4 minutes. Stir in the brown sugar, cinnamon, and sea salt to taste, and stir for another 30 seconds or so, until the mixture is well browned. Transfer to a paper towel–lined plate.

When the grill is hot, brush the cooking grates clean. Add the peaches skin side up and grill for 6 to 9 minutes, turning once after 4 or 5 minutes, or until the peaches are well marked on both sides. Transfer the fruit to bowls and serve with a scoop of ice cream and a spoonful or two of the streusel on top.

3 large firm-ripe freestone peaches, halved and pitted
Canola oil, for brushing
3 tablespoons unsalted butter
1-inch-thick slab sourdough bread (about 2½ ounces), torn into tiny pieces to make about 1 cup bread crumbs
¼ cup sliced almonds
2 packed tablespoons light brown sugar
½ teaspoon ground cinnamon
Flaky sea salt
3 cups Brown Sugar–Vanilla Ice Cream (recipe follows)

Brown Sugar–Vanilla Ice Cream

Makes 1 quart

Prepare an ice cream machine for freezing (or if camping, pack all the necessary equipment!).

In a small saucepan, combine the cream and milk over medium-high heat. Use a small, sharp knife to split the vanilla bean in half lengthwise. Scrape the vanilla seeds into the pan and add the pod as well. Cook, whisking occasionally to break up the vanilla seeds, until you just begin to see bubbles around the edges. Set aside to cool for 5 minutes. Remove and discard the vanilla pod.

Set up a sieve and ice bath for cooling the ice cream base: Fill a large bowl with ice-cold water. Place another bowl inside of that and a fine-mesh sieve inside the top bowl. Set aside.

In a medium saucepan, whisk together the egg yolks and both sugars. Continue whisking until the mixture is a full shade lighter in color, about 1 minute. (You should be starting to sweat.) Whisk in the steeped cream, then set the saucepan over medium-low heat and cook for 4 to 5 minutes, scraping the pan continuously with a soft rubber spatula, until the foam and bubbles disappear and the mixture steams and thickens a little and begins to look nice and silky. (Do *not* let it boil!)

Strain the mixture immediately into the bowl set over the ice bath and let it cool, stirring frequently, until it reaches room temperature, about 15 minutes. Transfer the ice cream base to a lidded 4-cup container (such as a mason jar) and refrigerate until thoroughly chilled, at least 4 hours or overnight.

Process the ice cream according to machine instructions, then transfer the ice cream to a lidded container and serve immediately (for softer ice cream) or freeze for at least 1 hour (or up to 3 weeks) before serving for firmer ice cream.

2 cups heavy cream
1 cup whole milk
½ vanilla bean
6 large egg yolks
⅓ packed cup light brown sugar
⅓ cup granulated sugar
Pinch of kosher salt

DIY: HOW TO BUILD A CAMPFIRE

BUILDING A CAMPFIRE IS OFTEN THE BEST PART of a camping trip, but it's also the one that requires the most thought. Living in the heart of wildfire country, we take our fire safety very seriously. But we also really love the warmth of a live fire, especially when we're out in the wilderness. We've taught all our girls from a very young age how to start and manage campfires. They know to make sure that all the tinder, kindling, and firewood they find on our property is very dry, and what kind of tinder burns best. If it's a windy day, we skip the fire to make sure we aren't at risk of spreading embers. (We also have a dedicated old truck with a water tank on it that we always have ready in case of emergency during our long summer fire seasons.)

Before you start, check your local regulations to make sure you have a permit for building a fire if you need one. Always use or build a fire ring (about 3 feet in diameter is a good rule of thumb), or dig a fire pit, and make sure it's at least 15 feet from your tent or sleeping area. Always make sure your fire is snuffed out before going to bed or leaving the area. And above all, don't risk a wildfire: do not build a live fire when it's fire season.

First, find a good spot: Look for a place that's flat and level and free of any brush or vegetation that could catch fire. Also keep in mind that wind can carry embers and move your fire—or start a new one—so find a place that's blocked from strong gusts of wind and be aware of which direction the wind is blowing. Clear the space of any leaves, sticks, branches, or other debris. If there isn't a fire ring there already, make one by placing a bunch of large rocks in a 3-foot-diameter circle.

Make sure you have a large bucket of water and a shovel nearby. If the fire becomes too large, extinguish it or minimize it by pouring water over the fire and carefully shoveling dirt onto the flames.

Once you have established a way to extinguish the fire, place the tinder, such as a small pile of dry brush and leaves, in the center of the fire ring and arrange a few pieces of kindling around the tinder. (You can pile them up in a teepee shape, or arrange them in a log cabin-style square around the tinder.)

Light the tinder with a match or lighter (or using flint and carbon steel, if you're familiar with them). Blow gently on the tinder to encourage it to catch fire, or fan it gently, until both the tinder and the kindling are burning.

Permit, as needed
Fire ring
Plenty of water and a shovel, for extinguishing the fire
Tinder, such as dry brush or leaves, fire starter balls, or dryer lint (see Note)
Matches, lighter, or flint
Kindling (small dry twigs and sticks)
Dry firewood (thicker dried branches or logs)

➤➤

Once the first few small twigs and sticks begin catching fire, slowly add more kindling until you have a consistent flame. Leave space between pieces of kindling so the oxygen a fire requires to burn can get between each piece. Most people kill fires by adding too much wood all at once. Fire needs oxygen to grow!

Once the kindling is burning well, add the firewood—either in the teepee pattern or in a log cabin–style square around the kindling. Start with the smallest pieces of firewood, and once those are burning, move to the larger pieces.

Enjoy your fire! As long as you're around, keep slowly adding (or "feeding") new firewood to the campfire, keeping it to a manageable size. For cooking, the key is establishing good coals, which come from the larger pieces of wood once they have burned all the way down. It takes about 30 to 45 minutes to establish a fire with good coals that can be used for cooking. (I start cooking when I can't hold my hand about 3 inches above the flames for more than a count of three.)

Finally, extinguish your campfire. This might be the most important skill.

It's best to allow the fire to burn all the way down to ash. But if that is impossible, the best place to start is by drowning the fire with water to extinguish it. You want to drown all of the embers until they stop making a hissing sound.

Next, mix the ashes and embers with the soil and the dirt, using a shovel if necessary, stirring the embers after they're covered with water and making sure that everything gets wet. If you feel the coals or embers or any part of the burned wood with your hands and anything is still hot, you're not ready to leave your fire yet. Don't leave or go to bed until your fire is dead out.

NOTE: Dryer lint—the typically blueish fibers and fluff you scrape out of the lint trap after doing laundry—is extremely flammable. Adding a golf ball–size pile to the center of your tinder pile is an easy way to help the fire start.

RIVER FLOAT BURGER BAR

Menu for 12

WE WORK SO HARD to ensure that every single package of our dry-aged ground beef is going to produce the most flavorful meal for our customers. We strive for the same at Five Marys Burgerhouse. Brian makes sure we're serving nothing less than the best beef we can produce, with excellent marbling and a memorable flavor. We want every burger to impress our customers every time. We love to share them with friends and family on the ranch too. One of our favorite early-summer activities is floating the river—and nothing beats burgers after a river float.

The Scott River winds along our property's edge, separating our pastures from our neighbors' land. The river runs as long as there is snowmelt coming down from the mountains, which means some years it runs all or most of the summer, but typically by the middle of summer, the riverbed is pretty dry. When the river is still flowing swiftly, we pack up our inner tubes and spend a day on the water, splashing and dunking and generally enjoying the Scott Valley's summer beauty.

We start at the bridge just a mile or so upstream of our property and float past our neighbors' hay fields and along our pastures, until we see the secret tree growing sideways on our ranch—it signifies we're near the little sandy beach that's our take-out spot. Brian brings the quad to come pick us up along the riverbank, then we head back to the ranch to grill burgers and make an elaborate toppings bar for piling them up with all of our favorite things. The burgers taste even better than usual because we're water-tired and the sun is setting behind our group of friends, and because the meat is everything we've worked so hard for it to be.

MENU TIPS

If you need to streamline your preparation time, it's OK to purchase Caesar dressing or a few of the burger toppings—but you could also make all that a few days ahead.

BRIAN AND I HAVE LUNCH at the Burgerhouse most of our working weekdays, usually hunched across from one another over laptops as we plan for the next project or problem-solve the latest emergency. We have worked hard enough most days to earn a Burgerhouse special burger, served with two flame-kissed patties made with our dry-aged ground beef on a soft potato bun.

At home, when we make burgers, we usually only put one beef patty on each bun, but we still do it up in the condiments department. I love a good spicy sauce, but I also love to balance that out with a bit of sweetness. The recipes that follow outline my idea of an ideal burger: I start with a patty tinged with herbs and spice (our meat doesn't need much). I top mine with pickled onions, candied bacon, tomato jam, a piquant fig spread, and a hit of blue cheese. When I put out a burger bar for a crowd, I also place chopped iceberg lettuce, tomato, and pickles on the table, but do what you want. (The M5-Rubbed Crispy Kale on page 21? Try it.) It's your burger bar.

Note: The recipes that follow for some of my favorite toppings are meant to feed a crowd, but they can all be scaled up or down as needed.

ALL-AMERICAN BURGER BAR

Makes enough for 12 burgers

Prepare a hardwood fire for grilling, or heat a gas or charcoal grill to medium-high (about 450 degrees F).

Divide the beef into twelve ⅓-pound portions and form each into an approximately 4-inch round patty, placing them on a baking sheet as you form them. In a small bowl, mix together the kosher salt, red pepper flakes, rosemary, thyme, sea salt, and black pepper. Sprinkle the spice mixture evenly over the patties (about ½ teaspoon for each), and set aside at room temperature while the grill heats. Lightly butter the insides of each potato bun and set aside.

When the grill is hot, brush the cooking grates clean. Add the patties seasoned side up and grill (with the lid closed, if using a charcoal grill) for 6 to 8 minutes, turning once about halfway through, or until the patties are well marked on both sides. (Cook for 6 minutes for a pretty rare burger, or 8 minutes for medium.) About a minute before the burgers are done, add the candied bacon to each patty and top with any cheese, closing the grill's lid again to allow them to warm for 30 seconds to 1 minute. Transfer the patties to a platter. Add the potato buns to the grill cut side down, cover, and toast for about 30 seconds, or until warmed and just barely marked.

To serve, allow guests to build their own burgers with any of the toppings they prefer.

4 pounds ground beef
1 tablespoon kosher salt
2 teaspoons red pepper flakes
1 teaspoon dried rosemary
1 teaspoon dried thyme
1 teaspoon flaky sea salt
¼ teaspoon freshly ground black pepper
12 soft potato hamburger buns, split horizontally
Unsalted butter, softened, for the buns (optional)
Honey–Brown Sugar Candied Bacon (page 198)
Spiced Pickled Red Onions (optional, page 198)
Balsamic–Black Pepper Fig Spread (optional, page 198)
Pickly Sungold Tomato Jam (optional, page 199)
Blue Cheese–Yogurt Spread (optional, page 199)
Jannie's Burger Sauce (optional, page 199)
Additional toppings (such as cheese, lettuce, tomato, and pickles), if desired

MY FAVORITE TOPPINGS

Honey–Brown Sugar Candied Bacon

For sweet, chewy bacon with some background heat: Preheat the oven to 350 degrees F. Line a baking sheet with heavy aluminum foil and fit it with a wire rack (the gridded kind), then arrange **12 thick-cut slices (about 1 pound) hickory-smoked bacon** on the grate so the pieces overlap as little as possible. Bake for 15 minutes, or until the fat begins dripping into the foil and the bacon begins to shrink. Meanwhile, in a microwave-safe container or saucepan, stir together **⅓ cup warmed honey, ⅓ packed cup dark brown sugar, 1 teaspoon kosher salt, ½ teaspoon cayenne,** and **½ teaspoon coarsely ground black pepper**. When the bacon is ready, separate the slices to expose as much of each piece as possible, then drizzle the honey mixture evenly all over the bacon. (You may need to heat the mixture for 10 to 20 seconds in the microwave, or over low in a small saucepan for a minute or two, until it pours easily.) Bake again for about 20 minutes, or until the bacon is cooked through and just starting to crisp in places. Turn each piece over and bake for another 3 to 5 minutes, or until the bacon is mostly crisp. Spread out the bacon on a large piece of parchment to drain for a few minutes, then halve each slice crosswise before topping the burgers. (The bacon can be cooked ahead, refrigerated in a sealed container for up to 3 days, and reheated before serving—in this case, a minute or two in the microwave actually works well!) *(Makes 12 slices.)*

Spiced Pickled Red Onions

For pickled onions with a bit of sass for topping burgers, tacos, and sandwiches, or eating out of the jar: Halve and thinly slice **a large red onion** pole to pole, break apart the pieces, and stuff them all into a 4-cup mason jar or similar container. In a small saucepan, combine **1 cup red or white vinegar** (really, any vinegar will do), **1 cup water, 1 tablespoon sugar, 1 tablespoon kosher salt, 1½ teaspoons red pepper flakes,** and **1½ teaspoons dry mustard powder,** and bring to a boil, whisking to dissolve the sugar and salt. Carefully pour the mixture over the onions, press any that are sticking out down into the liquid, and cover. Let cool to room temperature, then use immediately or refrigerate for up to 3 weeks. *(Makes 1 quart.)*

Balsamic–Black Pepper Fig Spread

For a perfect burger spread or savory toast topping: In a medium saucepan, stir together **2 pounds roughly chopped small ripe Mission figs (from 2 generous pints), ½ cup balsamic vinegar, ½ cup water, ¼ teaspoon kosher salt,** and **freshly ground black pepper** to taste. Bring the mixture to a boil, then reduce the heat to low, cover, and cook for 10 minutes, or until the fig skins are soft. Using a fork or a potato masher, mash the figs as fine as you'd like, then increase the heat to medium and cook at a strong simmer, stirring frequently, for another 10 minutes or so, or until the spread is thick and a shade darker in color. Stir in **1 tablespoon sugar**; season to taste with additional salt, pepper, and sugar; and let cool. You can transfer the spread to a lidded mason jar and refrigerate for up to 1 week, or process it according to the jar manufacturer's instructions to make it shelf stable. *(Makes about 3 cups.)*

Pickly Sungold Tomato Jam

For an easy homemade substitute for ketchup that also has a little heat: In a medium sauce-pan set over medium heat, combine **2 pints (about 4 cups) juicy, ripe Sungold, cherry, or grape tomatoes** with **¼ cup extra-virgin olive oil**, **¼ cup water**, **2 thinly sliced cloves garlic**, and plenty of **kosher salt** and **freshly ground pepper**. Bring the liquid to a simmer, then cover and simmer for 15 minutes on medium-low, until the tomatoes release their liquid and begin to collapse. Continue cooking, uncovered, at a strong simmer for another 10 minutes or so, or until the mixture is thick enough that when you draw a line across the bottom of the pan with a rubber spatula; it takes a moment for the jam to come back together. Stir in **1 table-spoon sugar** and **1 tablespoon white vinegar** (plus **1 teaspoon red pepper flakes**, for a spicier version), cook for 1 more minute, then transfer to a pint-size mason jar, cover, and cool to room temperature. The jam can be refrigerated for up to 1 week. *(Makes about 1½ cups.)*

Blue Cheese–Yogurt Spread

For a spreadable blue cheese that gives punch without falling out of the burger: In a small mixing bowl, use a fork to mash together **4 ounces softened cream cheese** and **4 ounces blue cheese or gorgonzola crumbles** with **1 cup plain whole-milk Greek yogurt**, then season generously with **kosher salt** and **freshly ground black pepper**. Use immediately, or cover and refrigerate for up to 1 week. *(Makes about 2 cups.)*

Jannie's Burger Sauce

We have a pickle-spiked special sauce we serve with fries at Five Marys Burgerhouse, but this version is closer to what I grew up making with my mom, Jannie: In a small mixing bowl, stir together **¾ cup ketchup**, **¾ cup mayonnaise**, and about **1 tablespoon sriracha (or other chili-garlic sauce)**. Refrigerate in a lidded container for up to 2 weeks. *(Makes about 1½ cups.)*

THE ULTIMATE BURGER BUN

Before any burger restaurant can begin serving, it has to do some serious research to find the perfect bun. For Five Marys Burgerhouse, we thought we'd be making brioche in-house—and at first, we did. But over time, two things happened: First, we realized that while brioche may be the gold standard for high-end burgers, making them from scratch requires a huge amount of time and labor, and brioche buns go stale in a matter of hours, so the buns we were baking in the afternoon weren't as fresh as we wanted by the time the last late-night orders came in. Second, we realized that the buttery taste of the brioche was masking some of the flavor of our dry-aged beef. We switched to a soft potato bun, which doesn't overtake the meat but is still sturdy and satisfying. Our staff agreed that the new bun-patty combo was the clear winner.

BRIAN'S MOM, CLAIRE (known as Oma to the girls), loves to cook and never stops exploring in the kitchen. Even in her seventies, she's constantly vetting new magazine recipes and introducing us to interesting flavor combinations. One of the few dishes she repeats is her tangy German cucumber salad, which is a great staple for summer gatherings. Made with pickled white onions, sour cream, and plenty of fresh dill, it's the kind of refreshing side you might accidentally finish standing at the counter before dinner begins. My version uses mini cucumbers (because they don't require peeling or seeding) and apple cider vinegar.

OMA'S GURKENSALAT

Makes 12 servings

In a large colander, toss the cucumbers with the salt and set in the sink for 30 minutes. (It will seem like an outrageous amount of salt, but you'll rinse it off later. The salt draws some liquid out of the cucumbers so the salad doesn't get too watery.) In a small bowl, toss together the onion, vinegar, sugar, garlic, and a pinch of salt. Set aside for 30 minutes, stirring occasionally.

In a medium serving bowl, stir together the sour cream, dill, and plenty of pepper. Add the pickled onions and their liquid, picking out and discarding the garlic along the way, and stir to blend.

Rinse the cucumbers thoroughly—they should taste seasoned but not salty—and transfer them to a clean dish towel. Gently pat the cucumbers dry, then add them to the bowl, stir to coat, and season to taste with salt and pepper. Serve or cover and refrigerate for up to 24 hours.

2 pounds mini cucumbers, trimmed, halved lengthwise, and cut into ½-inch-thick half-moons
2 tablespoons kosher salt
¼ white onion, thinly sliced
⅓ cup apple cider vinegar
1 tablespoon sugar
2 cloves garlic, smashed
1 cup sour cream
2 tablespoons finely chopped fresh dill
Freshly ground black pepper

WE SERVE HAND-CUT THICK FRIES at the Burgerhouse, but at home, I find it easier to slice them crosswise into rounds and throw them into the fryer—and with a dedicated waffle-cutting tool (which cuts in a wavy line to make "crinkle cut" rounds), they get crisper without any sort of extra coating. This is a great use for our M5 Spice Rub (see page 21) if you want a salty sprinkle with a little kick.

SWEET POTATO WAFFLE FRIES

Makes 12 servings

Trim the ends off the sweet potatoes and use a waffle cutter to slice them into ¼-inch-thick rounds, rotating the potatoes 90 degrees after each cut.

In a large, heavy soup pot, Dutch oven, or deep fryer, heat the canola oil to 375 degrees F.

When the oil is hot, add a few handfuls of the sweet potatoes. (Dropping them in one at a time, like you're putting coins into an old-school parking meter, prevents splashing.) Fry, turning occasionally and stirring to redistribute, until browned on both sides, 4 to 5 minutes. Transfer the potatoes to a wire rack set over a paper towel–lined baking sheet to drain, and season immediately with sea salt and pepper. Repeat with the remaining potatoes, allowing the oil to come back up to temperature or adjusting the heat between batches. Serve immediately, or keep warm on a baking sheet in a 250-degree oven.

4 medium sweet potatoes
About 4 quarts canola oil, for frying
Fine sea salt and freshly ground black pepper

NOTE: If you'd prefer baked fries, you can also brush them with oil and cook them in the center of the oven at 425 degrees F until crisp, about 20 minutes, rotating the pan halfway through baking.

I LIKE A STATEMENT DESSERT as a fun surprise at the end of a great meal. This party-size tart—a sheet-pan affair with a cookie crust, a baked Meyer lemon–curd cream, and a flurry of fresh berries on top—is the kind of thing that makes conversations stop. Which is good, because it demands attention. While the lemon bar base can be made ahead, you really want to pile the fruit on top just moments before serving.

BERRY PARTY TART

Makes one 13-by-18-inch tart (16 servings)

Chill the crust as directed on page 242, about 2 hours or overnight. Using the large holes on a box grater, grate the chilled crust directly onto a 13-by-18-inch rimmed baking sheet, allowing the shavings to fall in an even layer as you go. (It's OK if you wind up with some larger crumbles.) Using your palms and fingertips, press the dough across the bottom and up about ½ inch on the sides of the baking sheet. (The dough will be very thin.) Refrigerate for 30 minutes.

Preheat the oven to 350 degrees F. Bake the crust on the middle rack for 15 to 20 minutes, or until evenly golden brown. Let cool to room temperature, about 45 minutes.

Once the crust has cooled, make the lemon cream: In the work bowl of a food processor, process 1½ cups of the sugar with the lemon zest for about 30 seconds, or until the mixture is sandy and the zest is evenly distributed. Add the eggs and blend for 30 seconds, then add 1 cup of the cream, the lemon juice, butter, and salt, and pulse just to combine. Remove the bowl from the machine, rap it on the counter a few times to release any air bubbles, and pour the lemon mixture directly onto the cooled crust. Very carefully transfer the baking sheet back to the oven and bake for another 15 to 18 minutes, or until the lemon cream is firm and set in the center and the edges just begin to brown. Transfer the pan to a rack to cool for about an hour. (You can make the tart up to this point and leave it out at room temperature for up to 6 hours.)

In a large mixing bowl, toss the strawberries and blueberries with ¼ cup of the sugar and set aside for about 10 minutes to get juicy.

In a stand mixer fitted with the whisk attachment (or using an electric hand mixer), whip the remaining 2 cups of the cream with the remaining 2 tablespoons sugar on high speed until stiff peaks form, 1 to 2 minutes.

To serve, spread the whipped cream evenly over the lemon cream. Spoon the berries evenly across the top, arranging them as needed to cover, then press the berries down gently. Cut the tart into 16 or more rectangles and serve immediately.

1 recipe Homemade Ranch Animal Cookies dough (page 241), chilled

1¾ cups plus 2 tablespoons sugar, divided

2 tablespoons lemon zest (from 3 large Meyer lemons)

12 large eggs

3 cups heavy cream, divided

¾ cup freshly squeezed Meyer lemon or regular lemon juice (from 4 large lemons)

6 tablespoons (¾ stick) unsalted butter, melted

½ teaspoon kosher salt

2 pounds fresh strawberries, hulled, halved if large, and sliced

2 pounds fresh blueberries, blackberries, or raspberries

DIY: INDIGO TEA TOWELS

WHEN WE FIRST STARTED HAVING VISITORS on the ranch for retreats, we often incorporated crafts into the weekends. One of our favorites has been using indigo, the plant-derived dye well known for making blue jeans, to dye kitchen tea towels. Blue jeans and ranch life go hand in hand, and I'm always game for experimenting with new crafts.

Over time, playing with indigo dye led me to *shibori* dyeing techniques. Shibori—from a Japanese word that translates to "wringing" or "squeezing"—is a centuries-old Japanese fabric-making tradition. Like other ancient dyeing traditions from around the world, it commonly uses natural indigo. (Indigo played such a big role in ancient global trade routes that it was once referred to as "blue gold.") And while professional shibori is real art, it's also a great DIY project to take on at home. When we have visitors or family at the ranch, we often make shibori-inspired napkins, hand towels, or flags, and use them for table decoration for parties. In our restaurant's little retail corner, I started selling our indigo tea towels, marked with the M5 brand in fabric paint, and they were a hit. Here, I've distilled for you how I make the towels, which you can leave plain or paint as you'd like.

The modern indigo-preparing process takes some attention to do right, but it's so worth it for the deep-blue dye it produces because the color stays pretty consistent even after many washes. You need dried indigo dye or indigo paste, slaked lime, and powdered iron, which you mix together with hot water and let sit overnight before dyeing. While you can source each of these ingredients individually, I've found it's easiest (and most successful) to purchase them together in an indigo shibori-dyeing kit meant just for home use. Look for the kind that includes the ingredients above rather than those that just include synthetic indigo-colored fabric dye (which won't have quite the same hue or brightness and fades much more easily). Follow the instructions as precisely as you can.

Once the dye is ready, it's time to tap into your creativity. With shibori, there are different Japanese terms for folding, twisting, and pressing fabric between pieces of wood to make specific patterns. When you purchase an indigo-dyeing kit, it will likely come with instructions for making lattice, stripe, chevron, swirl, and tortoise-shell patterns. These are all gorgeous and super satisfying, but I've found that there aren't many sources for more basic designs—and the simpler patterns are the ones I like best. The steps that follow will walk you through the six shibori patterns I make most on the ranch. Follow them or branch out on your own!

⟶

Makes 24 tea towels

1. TRIANGLE FOLD
Pattern: Spotted blue-and-white pattern

Spread out a water-dampened towel in front of you on a flat work surface. Fold two opposite corners together to form a triangle, then repeat with the two corners farthest from each other, forming a second, smaller triangle. Repeat four more times, for a total of six folds, folding the two corners farthest from each other together each time and keeping the edges aligned as you work. You'll end up with a tight triangular bundle. To dye, dip half of the triangle (one short side and half of the longest side) into the indigo, hold for the length of time desired, then process per the indigo kit's instructions. (Dipping the more tightly folded side will produce a white background with blue spots; dipping the side with loose edges will produce a blue background with white spots.)

2. FAT STRIPE FOLD
Pattern: Fat blue-and-white stripes

Spread out a water-dampened towel in front of you on a flat work surface. Fold the towel in half by bringing the top edge down to meet the bottom edge. Fold it in half again, this time folding the left edge over to meet the right. Fold three more times, alternating the direction of the fold each time: fold the top to meet the bottom, the left to meet the right, and the top to meet the bottom again. You'll have a rectangular bundle of cloth, with the last fold at the top. To dye, dip the left half of the piece (for 3 white stripes and 2 blue stripes) or the right half of the piece (for 3 blue stripes and 2 white stripes) into the indigo, hold for the length of time desired, then process per the indigo kit's instructions.

3. GINGHAM SQUARE FOLD
Pattern: Blue-and-white checkerboard

Spread out a water-dampened towel in front of you on a flat work surface. Fold the towel in half by bringing the top edge down to meet the bottom. Fold it in half again, this time folding the left edge over to meet the right. Fold two more times, alternating the direction of the fold each time: fold the top to meet the bottom, the left to meet the right. You'll have a square of folded cloth. To dye, dip each straight edge about 1 inch into the indigo, hold for the length of time desired on each side, then process per the indigo kit's instructions.

1 complete indigo shibori-dyeing kit, plus any equipment it requires
24 (28-inch-square) cotton flour-sack hand towels
Thick rubber bands, for making designs in the fabric
Dishwashing gloves

NOTE: There's no such thing as shibori that doesn't "come out right." Embrace a *wabi-sabi* approach to dyeing, which is that all imperfections can be appreciated, and whatever happens is what was meant to happen. Sort of like ranch life!

RIVER FLOAT BURGER BAR

209

4. STARBURST BANDING
Pattern: Blue-and-white swirls

Spread out a water-dampened towel in front of you on a flat work surface. Pick a spot at random on the towel and use your fingers to twist the fabric into a tight spiral two or three times—like the start of a tie-dye swirl—so you end up with a wad of twisted fabric about as big as a golf ball. (The bigger the wad you make, the bigger the final swirl will be.) Wrap and bind the wad tightly with a thick rubber band, then repeat as many times as you'd like across the towel, making slightly different-size bunches of fabric, if you want more variation. (The more twisted wads, the more white space on the finished towel.) Don't forget to do a few swirls near the edges. To dye, dip the entire piece into the indigo, hold for the length of time desired, gently squeezing the fabric under the surface to encourage the dye to seep all the way into the center of the wads, then process per the indigo kit's instructions.

5. BANDED STRIPE ROLL
Pattern: Blue with thin white stripes

Spread out a water-dampened towel in front of you on a flat work surface. Starting from any side, roll the fabric up from one edge to the other, taking care to keep the edges aligned as you roll. Using thick rubber bands, tightly bind the fabric at roughly equal intervals along the rolled towel (the more rubber bands you use, the more white stripes there will be), twisting the rubber bands as tightly as you can each time for the whitest stripes. To dye, dip the entire piece into the indigo, hold for the length of time desired, gently squeezing the fabric under the surface to encourage the dye to seep all the way into the center of the roll, then process per the indigo kit's instructions.

6. ACCORDION FOLD
Pattern: Blue-and-white diamonds

Spread out a water-dampened towel in front of you on a flat work surface. Working from any edge, fold a roughly 5-inch strip of the fabric over onto itself. Fold four more times, switching the direction of the fold each time and taking the previous folds with you as you work to make an accordion pattern, until you have a long strip of five layers of fabric of equal width. (Think of making a folded paper fan: the actual width of each strip depends on the total size of your fabric, so adjust accordingly to make each fold the same.) Working in the opposite direction, fold the fabric five times again accordion-style so you have a small square of folded fabric. To dye, dip half of the square diagonally (from any side) into the indigo, hold for the length of time desired, then process per the indigo kit's instructions.

TIPS:

- It is helpful to wash and dry the fabric before dyeing.
- Always dip the fabric in water to moisten it, then wring it dry, before folding.
- Oxidation weakens the dye, so always keep a lid on it when you're not actively using it.
- Set a stopwatch for how long to hold the fabric in the dye for consistent results; most people tend to hold the fabric in the dye for less and less time as the project progresses.
- If after a few minutes in the air the fabric still shows spots of green, rinse out the green portions immediately.
- Indigo dye can stain skin, wood, clothing—anything, really. Wear long dish gloves to prevent turning your fingers and arms a new shade of blue.

PACK-AHEAD RODEO PICNIC

Menu for 6

RODEO EVENTS ARE GOOD TRAINING for our girls because they learn the skills they'll need to help corral or doctor the animals on our ranch. But when we started rodeo, what we didn't quite anticipate was their enthusiasm for competitions and their commitment to it. With the help of a neighboring family that really knows the sport, our girls have learned to compete in barrel racing, pole bending, breakaway roping, team roping, and calf riding.

When the girls started to compete in rodeos a few hours away from the ranch, rather than hauling a horse trailer to every event and packing all our camping stuff, we purchased a used LQ ("living quarters") trailer, which can house both horses and people in two separate compartments and has a tack room in between. It's quite the production—it is a beast of a trailer, weighing about 20,000 pounds! I remember seeing them on the road long before we imagined buying one and thought, "Wow, now *that* is a trailer!"

Inside, the LQ has a little dinette that turns into a bed and doubles as sleeping space, plus a queen bed and three bunks, so we all fit very comfortably (for trailer living). It has a small kitchen too—just a fridge/freezer combo, a microwave, and a two-burner stove, all within arm's reach of each other. But most of the time when we're at rodeos, we cook on a grill or a live fire and set up a camp kitchen right outside the trailer.

In the evenings, we try to plan a fun dinner with the friends we've made as the rodeo circuit weaves up and down rural California and Oregon. We bring a big old metal barrel and light a fire in the bottom, then hang tri-tips over the flames to cook as the sun goes down. Or if we can't have live fire because it's fire season, we make chili in a Dutch oven and keep it warm in a slow cooker until the rodeo is done for the day.

But during the competition, because we have four girls who each participate in multiple events, everyone is running different directions around lunchtime. Some days I'll make the girls a tray with cheese, crackers, veggies, nuts, salami and other cured meats, and fruit, so they can graze as they walk back and forth to the trailer to change horses or saddles or grab a different rope. If I have the time, though, I prepare more interesting picnic makings one of the days. For example, my hearty beef pasties are perfect make-ahead picnic food (and stay flaky even after a night or two in the fridge), and they guarantee everybody gets a good lunch between events.

While a pasty is plenty for me for lunch (they're big!), rodeo days are usually long, which means having snacks around is a must. I pack homemade apple chips (page 222) and crunchy quick pickles (page 221), and I always have a plan for a good cold cocktail when we wrap up.

MENU TIPS

Think of these recipes as a guide for planning a great picnic. Make the beef pasties, the apple chips, and the cocktail syrup before leaving home. When it's time to eat, you'll have a great handheld meal with zero assembly required.

SUMMER RODEO DAYS ARE LONG and often hot. I usually volunteer as a timer for the team roping competition, and when my shift is done, signaling the end of the day, I'm ready for a cold beverage. I love these spritzers, which have a sweet-tart syrup I whip up before we leave home. I usually double or triple the syrup so that all weekend long the kids can make their own cherry-fied version of a sparkling limeade and I can offer adult friends a fun twist on a gin and tonic without needing to set up a bar!

If you want a grown-up drink but just don't want the alcohol, skip the gin and just mix the syrup with tonic water.

CHERRY SPRITZERS

Makes 8 drinks

To make the syrup, in a small saucepan, combine the cherries, water, and sugar. Bring to a boil over high heat, then reduce the heat to low and simmer for 15 minutes, stirring occasionally. Remove the syrup from the heat, strain it into a jar, and stir in the lime juice to taste. Let cool to room temperature. (You should have about 1 cup.)

To make cocktails, in each of eight 12-ounce glasses filled with ice, stir together 2 tablespoons gin and 1 to 2 tablespoons of the cooled syrup. Add tonic to taste, stir, and serve with lime wedges.

To make kid drinks, fill each of eight 12-ounce glasses with ice. Add 2 tablespoons of the syrup (or to taste), then fill the rest of each glass with soda water and garnish with a lime wheel.

FOR THE SYRUP
¾ pound (about 2 cups) fresh or frozen cherries, smashed with the side of a knife, pits removed
1 cup water
⅓ cup sugar
¼ cup freshly squeezed lime juice (from 2 or 3 medium limes)

FOR COCKTAILS
1 cup gin
Tonic water
Lime wedges

FOR KID DRINKS
Soda water
Lime wheels

WHEN I MADE THESE MEATY BRITISH-INSPIRED HAND PIES and shared the recipe on Instagram, people raved—and it's no wonder! Wrapping our ground beef with tons of veggies in a flaky pastry crust makes a fun all-in-one meal that pleases everyone. The best part, in my opinion, is that they're durable enough to travel well. Now I bake them ahead of time and take them to rodeos, where busy days competing often mean we can't eat together midday. The girls can grab one when they're hungry and I know they'll be powered for events late into the evening.

GROUND BEEF PASTIES

Makes 6 pasties

To make the filling, in a large, heavy skillet over medium heat, melt the butter. Add the onion, celery, and carrot, season with salt and pepper, and cook, stirring frequently, until the vegetables begin to soften, about 5 minutes. Add the potato and rutabaga, and cook and stir for another 10 minutes or so, until all the vegetables are tender and browned in spots. Stir in the garlic and paprika, season again with salt and pepper, and cook another minute or two, until the mixture is fragrant. Transfer the vegetables to a medium mixing bowl and set aside.

Return the pan to the stove over medium-high heat. Add the beef, season with salt and pepper, and cook, breaking up the meat as you stir, until browned, crumbly, and cooked through, about 5 minutes. Transfer the meat (and any accumulated juices) to the bowl with the vegetables, mix well, and season to taste. Let cool to room temperature (then proceed, or to work ahead, refrigerate, covered, for up to 3 days).

To make the pasties, preheat the oven to 400 degrees F and position a rack in the center of the oven. Line a baking sheet with parchment paper and set aside.

Cut each dough disc into 3 equal portions (roughly 4 ounces each) and roll each portion into a ball. (If the dough has been chilling overnight, you may need to let it come to room temperature for 15 to 30 minutes before it's soft enough to roll.) Working with a floured rolling pin on a lightly floured board or work surface, roll each ball into an 8-inch round approximately 1/8 inch thick.

2 tablespoons unsalted butter
1/2 large yellow onion, finely chopped
2 medium celery stalks (about 3 ounces), diced
1 medium carrot (about 3 ounces), diced
Kosher salt and freshly ground black pepper
1 small russet potato (about 1/2 pound), peeled and diced
1 medium rutabaga (about 6 ounces), peeled and diced
2 cloves garlic, minced
1/2 teaspoon paprika
1 pound ground beef
1 recipe All-Purpose Double Pie Crust (page 166), made without sugar, chilled in 2 discs
1 large egg beaten with 1 tablespoon water
Flaky sea salt
Ketchup, for dipping (optional)

➤

Arrange the dough rounds on a large work surface. Divide the cooled filling among the six rounds (about ¾ cup per round), mounding it right in the center of each. Using a pastry brush, paint a 1-inch stripe of the egg wash around the perimeter of each round.

Working with one at a time, pick up a pastie and fold it in half like a taco, bringing the egged edges together to close the pastry around the meat. Hold the taco from the bottom in one hand and use the other to press the edges together and seal them. Gently return the pastie to the work surface and use a fork to crimp the sealed edges. Repeat with the remaining pasties.

Once all the pasties are crimped, use a small sharp knife (or better yet, a pizza cutter) to trim excess pastry from the crimped side about ½ inch from where the filling stops. (You can chill the pies at this point for up to 24 hours, loosely covered with plastic.) Brush the pasty tops with the egg wash, transfer them to the prepared baking sheet, and use the knife to make three 1-inch-long diagonal slits in the tops to allow steam to escape. Sprinkle the pasties with sea salt.

Bake the pies for 30 to 40 minutes, rotating once halfway through cooking, until deep golden brown and steaming. Serve warm or at room temperature with ketchup for dipping, or let cool to room temperature and refrigerate, then serve cold. You can also reheat chilled pasties for 5 to 10 minutes at 400 degrees F before serving.

I LOVE THE TANG OF PICKLED VEGETABLES on almost anything. I frequently have a jar of pickled onions in my fridge for burger or salad toppings (see page 198), and this combination of carrots, radishes, and jalapeños is quickly becoming a staple. Crunchy, sweet, spicy, and sour all at once, they're a great side for any sandwich but especially good with beef pasties on a hot day.

QUICK CARROT, RADISH, AND JALAPEÑO PICKLES

Makes about 4 cups

Pile the radishes, carrots, and jalapeños into two pint-size mason jars, mixing up the vegetables as you go. Set aside.

In a small saucepan, combine the vinegar, water, sugar, and salt and bring to a boil over medium heat. Cook, stirring, until the sugar and salt have dissolved completely. Divide the mixture among the jars, adding enough liquid to each to cover the vegetables completely. Press the vegetables down under the liquid to submerge them, if necessary, then screw on the lids and let cool to room temperature, about 2 hours. Serve immediately or refrigerate for up to 2 weeks.

1 (10-ounce) bunch radishes, greens and ends trimmed, peeled, halved lengthwise if more than 1 inch in diameter, and cut into ⅛-inch-thick rounds or half-moons

2 medium carrots (about 8 ounces), peeled and cut into ⅛-inch-thick rounds on a diagonal

2 large jalapeños, cut into ⅛-inch-thick rounds on a diagonal

1¼ cups unseasoned rice vinegar

⅔ cup water

¼ cup sugar

1 tablespoon kosher salt

WHEN THEY GET TOO OLD to saddle up or the girls outgrow their speed, our horses get to retire out on pasture. They quickly grow accustomed to their lives of leisure and are sometimes a little ornery about being caught to get their hooves trimmed or teeth worked on. Streak is one of our retirees. Once an old racehorse who lived up to his name, he now moves at a sloth's pace, with no intention of speeding up for anyone. When it's time to bring him in, our girls know to tuck an apple into their pocket to use as a bribe when they need to put on his halter. And since they usually have apples hiding in their pockets, the girls love snacking on them also—in any form!

These crispy baked apple chips are super easy to make and a great portable snack for riding (or bribing horses). I keep a jar of them on my rodeo table for the girls to grab in handfuls between events as they jump back on their horses to head over to the competition rings.

Note: If you don't have three baking sheets and three oven racks, just use two sheets and two racks, and make two apples' worth instead. If you want chewy dried apples, instead of crisp chips, increase the thickness to ¼ inch.

CRISPY BAKED APPLE CHIPS

Makes 6 snack servings

Preheat the oven to 200 degrees F. Line three baking sheets with parchment paper and evenly space three racks in the oven.

First, core the apples so you can see all the way through their centers vertically and no seeds remain. Using a mandoline, slice the apples into ⅛-inch-thick rounds. (Alternatively, with a knife, cut the apples in half vertically, core them, then cut into ⅛-inch-thick half-moons—it's easier to get the thickness right this way if you don't have a mandoline.)

Spread the slices from each apple onto one of the sheets, arranging them in four rows and allowing them to overlap slightly as needed—they will shrink during cooking, and will all fit on the sheet without touching eventually.

Bake for 1 hour, then gently separate the slices as much as you can, rotate the pans, and bake for another hour. Rotate and separate again, flip the slices over, and bake as long as needed until they become crisp, another 30 to 60 minutes. (The water contents of apples vary greatly, so the baking time will really depend on the type and condition of each apple you're using and exactly how thick you slice them.) To test the chips, remove a slice from each sheet and set aside to cool, about 2 minutes. If they're crisp, they're done!

Let the chips cool to room temperature, then munch away or store in a sealed container for up to 5 days.

3 medium tart apples (such as Granny Smith, Pink Lady, or Honeycrisp)

M5 FAMILY BIRTHDAY DINNER

Menu for 6

ONE OF OUR FAVORITE BIRTHDAY TRADITIONS in the Little House is to decorate the dining room table so that when the celebrant wakes up, she gets a fun surprise of decorations and gifts. Planning starts days in advance, with trips to the party drawer, where we keep streamers and banners and all sorts of other celebratory odds and ends. While the birthday girl sleeps, the others get to work, and nothing is off-limits—our eating nook gets piled with stuffed animals, birthday signs, and drawings. The table reveal is a tradition we all love, and paired with a treat breakfast like cinnamon rolls or pancakes (and protein—always protein!), it starts the day off just right.

In the evening, we usually have family and neighbors over for a celebration; birthdays are otherwise just another day on the ranch. Sometimes there's a piñata or balloons, but we always break out Five Marys pork chops, which the girls love but we save for special occasions, and also make something special for the girls to drink—often lemonade, tinted fuchsia with blackberries from our patch down by the river and sweetened with our own honey.

But the girls' favorite part is typically the cake. They get the same cake I had growing up: a casual but pretty angel food cake smeared lightly with raspberry-studded whipped cream. All of my childhood, my mom put the famous pink-and-white sprinkled store-bought animal cookies around the base of the cake so it looked like they were dancing after one another in a circle. It's simple, but the little carousel is as magical for our girls as it was for me growing up. Now, if we have time, our family makes the animal cookies from scratch—they taste extra delicious when they are homemade!

MENU TIPS

This is a generous menu for six people. If you have a bigger group, increase the number of chops as needed as the party grows. With more pork, the menu will stretch to ten people if you add an appetizer or two; if you still need more, all the recipes can be doubled. If you'd like to work ahead, bake the cookies and make the lemonade base a day or two in advance. You can bake the cake ahead too. For dinner, grill all the components of the panzanella first. Cook the pork, then the beans, and assemble the salad while the pork rests. The cake is best if you assemble it right before candle time.

FIVE MARYS SELLS RANCH HONEY, and we usually have lots of beehive boxes around the ranch. An apiarist keeps the bees on our property and manages the hives for us. So his honey business runs on our land, and we benefit from it, buying his delicious honey and bottling it as our own.

One time, when I was remodeling the testing kitchen in the Big House, I found an incredible 14-foot-long set of antique drawers that I planned to use for pantry storage. Before I could refinish forty drawers' worth of hardware, part of our local beehive decided the drawers would make a good home. So our kitchen project suddenly depended on convincing a queen bee that my antique was not her forever home. (If there's one thing ranch life provides, it's a constant stream of surprises.)

With help from a neighbor, we transferred the bees into something called a flow hive, which is a newer style of small backyard hive that allows you to pour honey from a tap, rather than opening the hive to collect it. Now we have the antique drawers installed in my test kitchen, *and* our own honey on demand—perfect for sweetening things when we want deep honey flavor. And there's nothing better than lemonade sweetened with good honey. While it's great as regular lemonade, it's a superb summer chiller spiked with vodka for the adults. Just don't get the two confused!

Triple the ingredients for a crowd; it will last about a week in the fridge.

BLACKBERRY-HONEY LEMONADE

Makes 8 drinks or 6 cocktails

2½ cups cold water, divided
½ cup high-quality honey
12 ounces fresh or frozen blackberries (about 2 cups)
½ cup plus 2 to 3 tablespoons freshly squeezed lemon juice (from 4 or 5 large lemons), divided
Lemon slices, for serving (optional)
⅔ cup chilled vodka (optional)

In a small saucepan, combine ½ cup water and the honey and bring to a simmer over medium heat, stirring until the honey has dissolved. Add the blackberries and return to a simmer, then set aside, cover, and let cool for 15 minutes.

Strain the berry mixture into a medium bowl, using a soft spatula to smash and press on the berries to extract as much liquid as possible. Discard the solids, then stir in another ½ cup water and ½ cup of the lemon juice into the berry juice, and transfer the mixture to a 4-cup jar with a lid. (You should have about 2½ cups.) Add the remaining 2 to 3 tablespoons lemon juice to taste and refrigerate until chilled, about 1 hour. This is your lemonade base, so it should taste quite strong and sour.

For lemonade, add another 1½ cups water to the base, or enough to get 4 total cups of liquid. Fill eight 12-ounce glasses with ice, pour about ½ cup lemonade into each glass, and garnish with lemon slices.

For a cocktail, add the vodka to the base and stir to combine. Fill six 12-ounce glasses with ice, pour in the lemonade, and serve with lemon slices.

WHEN WE BUTCHER OUR HOGS, we prefer to cut porterhouse-style pork chops, which leave the yummy section of the tenderloin on the pork chop (just like a Porterhouse steak with the filet mignon portion). For looks, we leave the bones nice and long. It means we don't get as many tenderloins or baby back ribs, but we think it's worth the trade-off. Because our customers love them so much, pork chops for ourselves are a precious commodity in our house—something we save for special occasions. Which means that almost every time a birthday rolls around, the girls ask for pork chops and then gnaw on the bones until they're shining.

These chops are grilled simply and topped with a fruit compote fragrant with cumin, coriander, and thyme. Nectarines, peaches, apricots, and plums all work well here—any sweet fruit base adds so much to a pork chop.

BONE-IN PORK CHOPS WITH SPICED STONE FRUIT

Makes 6 servings

Prepare a hardwood fire for grilling, or heat a gas or charcoal grill to medium (about 400 degrees F). Bring the pork chops to room temperature, rub with the olive oil, season generously with salt and pepper, and set aside.

While the grill heats, combine the cumin, coriander, and mustard seeds in a dry medium skillet over medium heat. Toast them, shaking the pan frequently, until popping, fragrant, and nicely browned, 1 to 2 minutes. Transfer the seeds to a mortar and pestle to cool, then carefully add the apple cider to the hot pan. Bring the cider to a boil and cook until it reduces by about half, about 10 minutes.

Meanwhile, crush the seeds in the mortar and pestle until almost powdery (or use the end of a rolling pin to crush them in an unbreakable container). When the cider has reduced, add the spices, fruit, vinegar, thyme, red pepper flakes to taste, and salt and pepper to taste. Cook over medium heat for 6 to 8 minutes, stirring occasionally, until the liquid is starting to look syrupy and the fruit threatens to fall apart. Cover and set aside until ready to serve.

When the grill is hot, brush the cooking grates clean. Add the pork chops and grill for 10 to 12 minutes, turning occasionally, or until the chops are well marked on both sides, pink in the middle, and register 135 degrees F for medium-rare or 145 degrees F for well-done on an instant-read thermometer. Transfer the chops to a platter and let rest for 10 minutes. Serve hot, topped with the fruit and syrup, and garnished with a little extra thyme.

6 (12-ounce, 1-inch-thick) bone-in center-cut pork chops

2 tablespoons extra-virgin olive oil

Kosher salt and freshly ground black pepper

1 teaspoon whole cumin seeds

1 teaspoon whole coriander seeds

1 teaspoon whole mustard seeds

2 cups apple cider

1½ pounds firm-ripe stone fruit (such as 3 nectarines or peaches, or 5 apricots or plums), halved, pitted, and sliced

3 tablespoons apple cider vinegar

2 teaspoons chopped fresh thyme, or ½ teaspoon dried thyme, plus more for garnish

⅛ to ½ teaspoon red pepper flakes

OUR FAMILY'S GARDEN is reliably at its peak around two of my girls' birthdays, in the middle of September. While we have a short growing season—the ranch is at 2,775 feet in elevation—we make the most of it, planting tomatoes, corn, onions, and always plenty of greens. We put up pickles when we can, but mostly we just enjoy what we grow. For this salad, the best of late summer gets charred on a grill, then sits in a sharp vinaigrette for extra flavor before being tossed with king-size grilled croutons, sturdy escarole, and bacon.

TOMATO-CORN PANZANELLA SALAD

Makes 6 to 8 servings (as a side) or 4 as a meal salad

Prepare a hardwood fire for grilling, or heat a gas or charcoal grill to medium (about 400 degrees F).

While the grill heats, pile the corn, tomatoes, and onion quarters on a baking sheet and brush them on all sides with about 2 tablespoons of the olive oil. Season with salt and pepper and set aside.

Dump the bread cubes into a medium bowl, drizzle with the remaining 4 tablespoons olive oil, season with salt and pepper, then toss and squeeze the cubes until they're evenly coated with oil.

Brush the cooking grates clean. Add the vegetables to the grill and cook for 8 to 10 minutes, keeping the lid closed as much as possible, turning everything every 2 or 3 minutes, or until the corn is marked on all sides, the tomatoes are browned and bursting, and the onion is charred on all sides. Transfer the vegetables back to the baking sheet and set aside to cool slightly.

Add the bread to the grill and toast until well browned on all sides, 6 to 8 minutes total, turning frequently. Return the bread to its bowl.

Meanwhile, in a large bowl, make the vinaigrette: Whisk together the vinegar, Dijon, and salt and pepper to taste until blended. Whisking constantly, add the olive oil in a slow, steady stream, then whisk in the cream and season to taste with more salt and pepper.

When the onions are cool enough to handle, cut them into thin slices and add to the bowl with the dressing. Cut the corn off the cobs and add it and the tomatoes to the bowl too. (You can pause here and refrigerate the vegetables for an hour or two, if you'd like, just until you're ready to serve, leaving the grilled bread at room temperature.)

To serve, add the bread to the vegetables and toss well to combine so that the bread soaks up plenty of the vinaigrette. Add the escarole, herbs, and bacon and toss again. Serve the salad family style or in large, shallow bowls topped with more herbs, if desired.

FOR THE SALAD
2 corn cobs, husked
1 pint cherry or grape tomatoes
1 red onion, quartered through its poles
6 tablespoons extra-virgin olive oil, divided
Kosher salt and freshly ground black pepper
4 cups 1-inch sourdough bread cubes (from about half a 2-pound loaf)
1 (8-ounce) head escarole, chopped (about 6 cups), or 6 cups chopped crisp greens
½ cup chopped fresh basil, tarragon, or parsley (or even better, a mix of the three), plus more torn herbs for serving
8 ounces sliced bacon, cooked and chopped

FOR THE VINAIGRETTE
½ cup red wine vinegar
1½ tablespoons Dijon mustard
Kosher salt and freshly ground black pepper
¾ cup extra-virgin olive oil
2 tablespoons heavy cream (optional)

VEGETABLES, LIKE CHILDREN, don't always need all the attention you can give them. That's certainly the case with green beans, which make all of us really happy with just butter and flaky sea salt. My favorite green bean recipe isn't really a recipe at all, but it sort of uses two cooking methods: the beans are cooked in butter in a cast-iron skillet on the grill, which means they get both the tiny bit of char you'd expect from a hot pan and, since they're trapped in a closed grill, the tenderness achieved from steaming.

SKILLET-GRILLED GREEN BEANS WITH BUTTER AND SALT

Makes 6 servings

Preheat a hardwood fire for grilling, or heat a gas or charcoal grill to medium (about 400 degrees F).

When the grill is hot, put a large cast-iron skillet on the grill grate and add the butter. When it is melted, add the green beans and toss to coat. Cover the grill and cook for about 10 minutes, tossing the beans every few minutes with tongs, until they are cooked al dente and browned in spots. Scrape them onto a serving plate, shower with sea salt, and serve hot.

2 tablespoons unsalted butter
1½ pounds green beans, trimmed
Flaky sea salt

OUR FAVORITE TRADITIONAL BIRTHDAY CAKE is one I've heard many others remember from their childhoods too: a gloriously fluffy angel food cake topped with raspberry-tinged whipped cream and decorated with sprinkles and animal cookies. Our level of involvement changes from year to year depending on what's happening on the ranch. If we have a houseful of late-summer bottle-feeding calves to nurse around the September birthdays, it might mean buying the cookies, but if we can, we make it all from scratch, right down to choosing which ranch-themed cookie cutters to use.

Every time I make it, I am reminded how quickly angel food cake comes together. Frequently, I think, people avoid making it from scratch because the recipe relies on cream of tartar, which contributes acidity that helps solidify the structure of the cake—but it's not used all that much in modern baking, so it's often something people don't have on hand. This recipe calls for lemon juice instead, which does the same job and also adds a little more flavor. Cooling the cake completely while it's upside down isn't optional; it's crucial if you want the cake to hold its structure.

CAROUSEL ANGEL FOOD BIRTHDAY CAKE

Makes one 10-inch cake

Preheat the oven to 375 degrees F. Set out an ungreased 10-inch angel food cake pan. (Nonstick pans are OK, but do not grease the pan in any way. If your pan has a removable bottom, place the pan on a baking sheet.)

First, make the cake: In a medium bowl, whisk together the cake flour and lemon zest and set aside.

In the bowl of a stand mixer fitted with a whisk attachment (or in a very large mixing bowl, using an electric hand mixer), whisk the egg whites, lemon juice, vanilla, and salt together on high speed until soft peaks form, 1½ to 2 minutes. With the mixer running, add the sugar in a slow, steady stream, whisking for another 30 seconds or so, until the mixture is stiff and beginning to look glossy.

Sprinkle in about half of the flour mixture, then use a flexible spatula to gently fold in the flour. Add the remaining flour and continue folding until no visible streaks remain.

Scoop the batter into the ungreased pan, smooth it out with the spatula, and rap the pan on the counter a couple times to release any big air bubbles. Bake for about 30 minutes, or until the cake is browned on top and a skewer inserted into the center comes out clean.

FOR THE CAKE
1½ cups cake flour, sifted
2 teaspoons lemon zest (from 1 large lemon)
12 large egg whites, at room temperature
1 tablespoon freshly squeezed lemon juice
½ teaspoon vanilla extract
½ teaspoon kosher salt
1½ cups sugar

FOR THE WHIPPED CREAM
1¼ cups cold heavy cream
2 tablespoons sugar
Pinch of kosher salt
6 ounces (1 scant cup) fresh raspberries

FOR DECORATING
Store-bought animal cookies or Homemade Ranch Animal Cookies (page 241)
Small rainbow nonpareil sprinkles

➡

Remove the pan from the oven and immediately flip it upside down. (If your pan has metal prongs that elevate it above the counter when flipped, great. If not, place the pan over a wire rack so air circulates underneath it.) Allow the cake to cool completely without disturbing, about 2 hours.

When the cake is cool, run a thin knife around the inner and outer edges of the pan, and invert it onto a serving plate. Set aside until ready to serve. The cake can be made up to a day ahead and stored at room temperature, covered with plastic wrap, until you're ready to decorate it.

Just before serving, make the whipped cream: In the bowl of a stand mixer fitted with a whisk attachment (or in a very large mixing bowl, using an electric hand mixer), whisk the cream on high speed until soft peaks form, about 2 minutes. Add the sugar and salt, whisk to blend, then add the raspberries and mix another 20 seconds or so, until the raspberries are slightly broken up and the cream shows smears of pink. Use a flexible spatula to fold the raspberries at the bottom into the rest of the cream, then spread the cream all over the cake. (You can shove any excess into the center!)

To decorate, we like to line up the animals around the base of the cake as if they're marching together in a carousel—and go wild with the sprinkles. Serve immediately. Store any uneaten cake in the refrigerator, covered lightly with plastic wrap; it will stay delicious for a few days, but the sprinkles will bleed their color into the cream.

NOTE: On the ranch, we have plenty of eggs already at room temperature. If you use refrigerated eggs for this recipe, allow about an hour for them to come to room temperature. Cold eggs don't hold as much air! Use some of the yolks leftover from this recipe for Brown Sugar–Vanilla Ice Cream (page 187).

HOW WE STORE EGGS ON THE RANCH

Did you know you only need to refrigerate store-bought eggs because they've been washed? It's true. Straight out of the nesting boxes, eggs are coated with a natural antibacterial coating called the bloom. When the bloom is left on, eggs remain fresh at room temperature for weeks or months, depending on humidity and the egg. Washing an egg removes the bloom, and allows the egg's shell to become porous, and more prone to spoiling—which is why we need to chill the eggs we buy at the store. We keep our ranch eggs in a bowl on the kitchen counter.

DIY: HOMEMADE RANCH ANIMAL COOKIES

THE ICONIC PINK-AND-WHITE ANIMAL COOKIES have always been a staple on our family's birthday cakes. One day, it occurred to me that I could just make them myself. I found some ranch-themed mini cookie cutters, and homemade ranch animal cookies became a thing in our house.

Since the dough is pretty resilient, these cookies are a great way to involve kids in making a cake that's otherwise best for adult hands. Ask even the youngest kiddos to help you soften the dough. The sprinkles are the best part (obviously!) but they're about as easy to clean up as glitter, so work over a rimmed baking sheet—or better yet, outdoors.

This recipe allows for plenty of icing in case you're working with little folks and want to divide it into a few bowls, but if you're a cookie pro, you can halve the icing amount. Similarly, if you only want to ice one side of the cookies (rather than both, as with the store-bought version), halve the icing.

For the food coloring, remind your helpers: you can always make it darker, but it's hard to go the other direction.

Note that these cookies aren't made with any preservatives, so it's best to ice them the same day you want to decorate the cake. You can bake the cookies themselves up to 3 days ahead, cool them, and store them at room temperature in an airtight container. Iced cookies will keep at room temperature, covered, for a few days.

Makes about 6 dozen 1- to 1½-inch animal cookies, depending on the cutters

Baby animal–shaped cookie cutters (about 1 to 1½ inches across)

2 or 3 baking sheets

2 wire racks (the gridded kind)

FOR THE COOKIES

1¾ cups all-purpose flour, plus more for rolling and cutting the dough

¾ teaspoon baking powder

¼ teaspoon kosher salt

1 stick (½ cup) unsalted butter, at room temperature

1 cup granulated sugar

1 large egg

½ teaspoon vanilla extract

FOR THE ICING

2 pounds (7½ cups) confectioner's sugar

½ cup hot water, plus more as needed

2 teaspoons vanilla extract

Pinch of kosher salt

About 2 ounces small rainbow nonpareil sprinkles

High-quality food coloring

⟶

To make the cookie dough, in a medium bowl, whisk together the flour, baking powder, and salt, and set aside.

In the bowl of a stand mixer fitted with the paddle attachment, mix the butter and granulated sugar on low speed until all the sugar is moistened. Increase the speed to medium and mix for 1 minute, or until the mixture is light and a little fluffy, scraping down the sides of the bowl as needed. Add the egg and vanilla and mix again on medium speed until the egg is totally incorporated, then add the dry ingredients. Pulse a few times to incorporate the flour, then mix on low speed until no white streaks remain. Transfer the dough to a piece of plastic wrap or waxed paper, press into a 1-inch-thick disc, wrap well, and refrigerate for 2 hours, or until firm. (You can also refrigerate the dough for up to 2 days. If your dough has been refrigerated longer than 2 hours, leave it at room temperature for about 30 minutes before proceeding.)

When you're ready to bake the cookies, preheat the oven to 350 degrees F. Unwrap the dough and break it in half, then rewrap one-half and set it aside.

Divide the dough half into four pieces. Knead each piece for about 15 seconds between your palms, until it becomes softer and no longer crumbly. Repeat with the other three pieces, then squish the dough back together and knead it into one soft ball. On a well-floured work surface, use a floured rolling pin to roll out the dough into a round about ⅛ inch thick and 9 inches in diameter. Cut the dough into whatever shapes you want and transfer to an unlined baking sheet. The cookies don't rise much, so you only need to leave about ½ inch of space between cookies. Reroll and cut any dough scraps, and reflour your work surface and rolling pin as needed to prevent the dough from sticking.

Bake the cookies for 10 minutes, rotating the pan halfway through, or until they are nicely tanned at their edges and browned on the bottoms. Let the cookies cool on the pan for 1 minute, then use a flat metal spatula to loosen them and transfer to a wire rack to cool for about 20 minutes. While the first batch bakes and cools, repeat the process with the remaining dough half.

When all the cookies have cooled, make the icing: In a medium heatproof bowl, whisk together the confectioner's sugar, ⅓ cup of the hot water, the vanilla, and salt. Add more water a little at a time until the icing loosens and is easy to stir (you might not need it all), then whisk until totally smooth. Bring a small saucepan filled with about an inch of water to a bare simmer while you work. (You'll need it again later.)

Dip the flat bottom of each animal cookie into the icing, let the extra icing drip back into the bowl, then set it iced side up on a wire rack (the gridded kind). (If the icing doesn't drip back into the bowl in a continuous stream right when you take the cookie out, it's too thick; add a tiny bit more water.) Add as many sprinkles as you want before the icing dries. (I find it works well to ice about 5 cookies, then sprinkle, then ice 5 more.) When about half the cookie bottoms are iced, stop the icing process and wait about 10 minutes. (The rest of the cookies will be iced later.) Before icing the other sides, rest the icing bowl on top of the simmering water for about a minute to rewarm, then whisk the icing to loosen.

Ice the tops of the cookies: Using the same method, dip the un-iced side of each cookie into the icing, let the excess drip off, and set the newly iced side up on the rack. Every 5 cookies or so, pause to sprinkle. When the cookies are fully iced and decorated, set them aside to dry for about 20 minutes.

Repeat the icing-warming process, then add food coloring to the remaining icing and whisk until uniform. (For a pink shade similar to store-bought animal cookies, I add 3 drops at a time, using 2 drops of red for every drop of pink, and continue adding in that ratio until I achieve the shade I want.) Repeat the icing process with the second batch of cookies, adding a tiny bit of hot water to the icing if it seems too thick and rewarming it between sides, until all of the cookies are iced and dry.

Using your fingertips, gently budge the cookies from their rack to unglue them and allow the icing that was touching the racks to dry. Let them sit for another 30 minutes, then serve as a snack or use for decorating the Carousel Angel Food Birthday Cake on page 237!

Fall

SEPTEMBER IS CALVING SEASON ON THE RANCH. Cows are pretty independent mommas—more independent than sheep, actually—but still, during the busiest weeks, we check on them multiple times a day and night, usually every few hours. As Brian likes to say, hope isn't an effective method of doctoring, so we have high standards for how we care for the cows and calves alike. At the crack of dawn, he's out in the foggy pastures, inspecting the heifers (first-time moms) for signs of readiness or distress, ear-tagging any calves that have been born overnight, and making sure all the newborns are nursing well and paired up with a mother cow. If there are babies that don't seem to be getting enough milk at first, he bottle-feeds them right there in the pasture to give them the best start possible.

Calving season winds down in October, and then we have branding day, typically in November, when we do a health checkup on all the animals and vaccinate and brand the calves. It's a long day that requires plenty of help from the neighbors (and they know it always ends with a hearty meal as a thank-you). Then the cycle starts again: in early December, we begin the process for animals we'll breed the next season.

Before and after calving, fall is also when Brian takes the girls deer hunting, hiking way up onto our land with them. In October, we have our annual Heffernan family weekend, when the cousins all camp out together on our ranch or a cousin's ranch. There's also roping practice—an excellent excuse for cooking an arena-side dinner on our huge tow-behind grill—and time spent lending a hand to other ranches on their own branding days. By the time the holiday season hits and we've gotten used to chopping wood for our stoves again, we're ready to dig into old family recipes.

BRANDING DAY DINNER

Menu for 6

WHEN WE DECIDED WE WOULD SELL OUR MEAT under the Five Marys name, we wanted our brand to incorporate the number 5 and the letter M. While that works well enough on paper, and for our family, branding cattle hides is a little different: brands wind up more distinct (and easier to see from a distance) if none of the lines change direction with less than a 45-degree angle. We came up with our M5 brand, made with a wavy M that connects to the 5, as a way of making the brand as legible as possible.

Every time we harvest cattle, a state brand inspector comes to the ranch to verify that all our animals bear the Five Marys brand on the left rib area. (Ranchers register both the look of the brand and the location where it is to be branded on their livestock.) It also guarantees that we haven't stolen the cattle and protects us in case someone steals ours; cattle rustling is something ranchers across the country still battle. Plus, it helps if the cows manage to break through our fences. They say a rancher whose cows have never gotten out is a rancher who doesn't own cows! Their identifying ear tags can fall out, and a brand is the only certain way to identify what ranch the cattle call home. At the Burgerhouse, we have a gallery wall with wooden blocks displaying the brands used in our valley. A family brand is a sacred thing.

We usually brand our new cattle in one day every November in an all-hands-on-deck effort that leaves us pretty exhausted. It's hard work, but because it involves a team of friends with everybody working together, it's one of our girls' favorite days on the ranch. At the end, we feed everyone who's helped—usually something simple but satisfying, like a huge sheet-pan dinner I can prep ahead and throw in the oven once the branding is done.

MENU TIPS

Because the rice takes the longest to cook, start that first. As the oven preheats, you can prep the pork and vegetables, then ready the pears (which are super easy) while the pork cooks.

OUR BRANDING DAYS ARE LONG. Brian likes to say that when we brand, he's always looking for a specific cow all day—the last one. At the end, we usually reward ourselves with a well-earned cocktail. Although my favorite is a sidecar, made with bourbon and Meyer lemons, it's something that has to be made fresh—and honestly, by the end of branding day, I want to *drink* a cocktail, not make one, before I even think about starting dinner. That's why I stir up these Manhattans a day or two ahead, going down into our root cellar for a bottle of the really good scotch that gives them just a hint of smokiness. Left in the fridge for a few days, the flavors have time to meld and mellow, which makes for an even better drink, in my opinion. And the cowboys helping with branding love them.

LONG DAY MANHATTANS

Makes 6 cocktails

Combine the bourbon, vermouth, whiskey, and bitters in a large mason jar and stir well. (You can refrigerate the mixture for up to a month.) Shake about a third of the mixture at a time over ice in a cocktail shaker, to make two drinks at a time, or shake one drink at a time in a pint-size mason jar filled with ice. Pour about ½ cup into each cocktail tumbler over fresh ice, or into martini or up glasses, if preferred. Garnish each drink with a cherry.

2 cups good bourbon, such as Five Marys Nothin's Easy Bourbon
¾ cup high-quality sweet vermouth, such as Carpano Antica
1 tablespoon high-quality aged scotch whiskey (such as Lagavulin or Laphroaig)
1½ teaspoons orange bitters
6 Homemade Cocktail Cherries (page 17)

AGING COCKTAILS FOR A CROWD

Believe it or not, these Manhattans are at their peak smoothness after about a month in the fridge. To age them for a crowd, start by tripling the recipe. In a large bowl or pitcher, combine the bourbon, vermouth, whiskey, and bitters, then whisk gently until thoroughly blended. Divide the mixture among 18 (8-ounce) mason jars, putting about ½ cup liquid in each, then screw the lids onto the jars and refrigerate for at least a week and up to a month. For a party, put the jarred cocktails in a cooler next to a bucket of ice and a bowl of cherries, and allow people to ice and garnish their own drinks! *(Makes 18 cocktails.)*

SHEET-PAN DINNERS ARE MADE FOR BUSY DAYS. It's great when they're flexible enough, like this one, that you can do any required chopping in advance, and it's also a relief to have roasted herbed pork tenderloin and plenty of golden-brown veggies but only one pan to clean. When I know I have a really hectic schedule—say, a morning of shipping, followed by a photo shoot, followed by an afternoon when I join the branding operation—I'll do my best to get a dinner like this into the fridge well before noon so that when the sun has finally set, I don't have to do much besides heat up the oven.

If you're feeding a crowd, you can double or triple the amounts, but cook each batch of the recipe on its own baking sheet. (Piling too much on one sheet will cause the vegetables to steam rather than roast.) Serve the dinner with a side of Perfect Wild Rice (page 257) or Icebox Pull-Apart Rolls (page 53), which can also both be made ahead.

SHEET-PAN PORK TENDERLOIN WITH DELICATA, KALE, AND BRUSSELS SPROUTS

Makes 6 servings

Preheat the oven to 400 degrees F. Place a baking sheet on the center rack and allow it to preheat as well.

To prepare the vegetables, put the squash, sprouts, and shallots in a large mixing bowl. Drizzle with 3 tablespoons of the olive oil, then add the garlic, thyme, and red pepper flakes to taste; season with salt and pepper; and toss to combine and coat all the vegetables in the oil and seasonings.

To prepare the pork, on a large cutting board, rub the tenderloins on all sides with 2 tablespoons of the olive oil, then season with the rosemary, salt, and pepper. Position the tenderloins together lengthwise in opposite directions so the fat end of one snuggles up to the thin end of the other and together they make one cut of meat of roughly even thickness along their lengths. Using butcher's twine or string, tie the tenderloins together snugly at 2-inch intervals. Trim off any extra string. (This method helps the tenderloins cook evenly. You can prep the vegetables and pork ahead of time and refrigerate, covered, for up to 8 hours before roasting.)

➡

1 large or 2 small delicata squash (about 1 pound), halved, seeded, and cut into 1-inch half-moons

1 pound large brussels sprouts, trimmed and halved

8 medium shallots, peeled and halved

7 tablespoons extra-virgin olive oil, divided

5 large cloves garlic, smashed

2 teaspoons chopped fresh thyme leaves

¼ to ½ teaspoon red pepper flakes

Kosher salt and freshly ground black pepper

2½ pounds pork tenderloins (2 large or 3 small)

2 tablespoons chopped fresh rosemary

2 medium lemons, halved and seeded

1 (8-ounce) bunch lacinato kale, large ribs removed, torn into 2-inch pieces

When the oven is hot, remove the baking sheet, place the pork in
the middle, and carefully spread the vegetable mixture around the
pork in a roughly even layer. Toss the lemon halves anywhere on the
pan and roast for 30 minutes.

Meanwhile, add the kale to the large bowl and drizzle with the
remaining 2 tablespoons olive oil, season with salt and pepper, and
toss to blend. Set aside.

After 30 minutes, remove the pan from the oven, scatter the kale
over the vegetables, and give them all a stir to incorporate the kale.
Roast for another 15 minutes or so, or until the pork registers 135
degrees F for medium-rare or 145 degrees F for well-done on an
instant-read thermometer inserted in the thickest part, and the
squash is completely tender. Remove the pan from the oven and let
everything rest for 5 minutes.

Serve the pork hot, directly from the baking sheet, slicing it as you
go, with the lemon halves squeezed over everything just before
serving.

WHILE CALIFORNIA AGRICULTURE MIGHT BE MOST FAMOUS FOR FRUIT, the state is also a leading producer of wild rice. There's a great rice-growing region not far from the ranch, in the shadows of Mount Shasta. In the fall especially, we love making earthy, chewy wild rice as a nutritious side dish that goes well with just about anything. For extra flavor and lots of healthy minerals, we simmer it with our nutrient-dense beef bone broth, which is slow-cooked over 24 hours. The girls can cook it themselves, and the rice makes great leftovers.

For multicooker rice, seal the pot, then pressure-cook on high for 30 minutes. Allow the pressure to release naturally for 10 minutes, then keep warm until ready to serve.

PERFECT WILD RICE

Makes 6 servings

To make the rice, in a medium saucepan, stir together the rice, broth, maple syrup, and salt. Bring to a boil over high heat, then reduce the heat to medium and simmer uncovered, stirring a few times, for 1 hour, or until the rice is just tender and beginning to split. Serve hot, using a slotted spoon so any excess liquid drains back into the pot.

1 cup (8 ounces) long-grain wild rice
4 cups beef bone broth
2 tablespoons maple syrup
½ teaspoon kosher salt

WE ENJOY A SMALL INDULGENCE after a great meal shared with friends, but usually a day on the ranch doesn't give us time to prepare a fussy dessert. That's why I love these sweet, earthy roasted pears. Unlike most pear desserts, this one doesn't require peeling or poaching or any sort of pastry—you just cut and core the pears, then dip them in cinnamon-sugar and slide them into the oven. Even the caramel, which comes together in the amount of time it takes the pears to soften, is quick. If you want to dress them up, top the warm pears with freshly whipped cream or Brown Sugar–Vanilla Ice Cream (page 187).

CINNAMON-SUGAR ROASTED PEARS WITH QUICK HONEY CARAMEL

Makes 6 servings

Preheat the oven to 400 degrees F and position a rack in the bottom third of the oven. Line a baking sheet with parchment paper and set aside.

On a small plate, mix the sugar with ½ teaspoon of the cinnamon. Dip the cut sides of the pears in the sugar, pressing down gently, then transfer the pears, sugared sides down, to the prepared baking sheet. (Reserve the remaining sugar mixture.) Roast for 10 minutes, or until the pear skins are tanned and the sugar browns around the edges of each pear.

Meanwhile, make the caramel: In a medium stainless steel saucepan, combine the honey, the reserved sugar, and the remaining ½ teaspoon cinnamon. Set over medium-high heat and cook, swirling the pan but not stirring, until the sugar melts and the honey darkens and just begins to smoke and bubble toward the top of the pan, 3 to 5 minutes. Remove from the heat and carefully whisk in the cream, then transfer the caramel to a small jar or pitcher.

Serve the pears warm or at room temperature drizzled with the caramel and sprinkled with sea salt.

½ cup sugar

1 teaspoon ground cinnamon, divided

3 firm-ripe Bartlett pears, halved lengthwise and cored

¼ cup honey

½ cup heavy cream

Flaky sea salt

FIVE-GENERATION RAVIOLI NIGHT

Menu for 8

ELLA ARNERICH, MY MATERNAL GREAT-GRANDMOTHER, came from Croatian parents but was born and raised in Amador County, in Northern California's gold country. My mom called her Nona. Her son, Jim Arnerich, was my grandfather. "Big Jim" was one of my favorite people in the world (and I like to think that as the oldest, I was his favorite grandchild). He used to drive me around town and we'd play a game where we invented businesses for retail spots that were for sale or vacant, imagining an ice cream shop here or a shoe shop there—a habit I now credit for my entrepreneurial spirit. When he visited, we'd make Nona's tender beef ravioli recipe with my mom, Janet Arnerich Simonson. The day before Big Jim died, I was at his bedside, where he made me promise to teach the future generations how to make Nona's ravioli. His old Italian pasta-rolling machine made its way to me when he passed, and now my girls are cranking away as at least the fifth generation of ravioli makers on my mom's side.

Today, the heart of the recipe lies on two sides of a tired index card from the '80s, written in blue ink that's bled to purple with age (and probably water damage). "Two sets beef brains" is still clearly legible under *From the kitchen of . . .* , with "Nona" written in my mom's signature handwriting. When I was growing up, like my ancestors, we used a combination of ground round steak and those brains, but today, both because brains aren't widely available and because our tastes have changed, we use ground lamb, which keeps the filling super moist and flavorful. We start by mixing and kneading a simple, silky-smooth pasta dough. Then we roll it out into ribbons so thin we can almost see through them; form and cut the ravioli (using my mom's special Italian ravioli-shaping rolling pin, if we're at her house); and boil them. They are then topped with a basic but delicious browned butter sauce, Parmesan cheese, and chopped fresh mint. Although the recipe has changed with the times, I think Big Jim would be proud. I hope my girls remember days in the kitchen making Arnerich ravioli and sharing family stories.

MENU TIPS

You'll find my mom's favorite way to make pasta dough on page 271. Start the ravioli process by cooking the onions and spinach, then while they cool, make the dough. While the dough rests, finish the filling, then roll out the dough and start assembling the ravioli.

Because the pasta-making process takes time, when I do it, I want the meal to focus on the ravioli. I serve it with the simplest arugula salad (my hands-down favorite way to serve arugula) and an easy egg custard. Make the ricotta appetizer and the custard ahead of time and serve them at room temperature.

THERE SEEMS TO BE AN INHERITED SIXTH SENSE that everyone has on my side of the family—one that tells us when something delicious is ready to eat. We even have a saying in our family that there are two kinds of people at the dinner table: the quick and the hungry. Good food goes fast in a crowd! When we get together, we gather around hot food like moths to light, everyone reaching at once.

This warm ricotta dip calls strongly to that sixth sense, and when it's ready, we all dig in and swoon with pleasure as one. But do give it time to rest, if you can—it's much more scoopable after it's cooled for a few minutes.

WARM RICOTTA DIP <u>WITH</u> OLIVES AND LEMON

Makes 8 servings

Preheat the oven to 350 degrees F.

In a medium mixing bowl, stir together the ricotta, olives, eggs, lemon zest, salt, and red pepper flakes to taste. Transfer the mixture to a 1-quart baking dish (or something just large enough to hold it all), smooth the top, and bake for about 35 minutes, or until puffed but still a bit jiggly in the center. Let the dip cool for 15 minutes before serving warm or at room temperature with crackers alongside.

1 (48-ounce) container whole-milk ricotta

1 cup pitted olives (such as Castelvetrano or kalamata, or a mix of the two), finely chopped

2 large eggs

Zest of 2 Meyer lemons

½ teaspoon kosher salt

¼ to ½ teaspoon red pepper flakes (optional)

Assorted crackers, for serving

SUPER-SIMPLE ARUGULA SALAD

My sister-in-law Emily makes this simple salad for family get-togethers often. It's so easy, but it's also the most delicious salad, and a perfect accompaniment to an otherwise more involved meal. Coating and lightly massaging the leaves with oil before adding lemon juice prevents the greens from wilting too quickly.

   In a salad bowl, massage 5 ounces baby arugula with 2 tablespoons extra-virgin olive oil until all the leaves are evenly moist. Add an entire small lemon's worth of juice (about 2 tablespoons)—or more if you like things super tart—then shower the leaves with flaky sea salt and freshly ground black pepper and mix again to blend. Serve immediately. *(Makes 6 servings.)*

FOR GENERATIONS, MY FAMILY MADE RAVIOLI with beef brains. At some point, eating brains fell out of favor in America, and we had a harder and harder time sourcing them. Once, when I was young, my dad was getting tired of calling around to find them. As the story goes, he decided to call one last butcher. Instead of asking for "beef brains" when someone answered the phone, my dad said, "Hey, do you have any brains?" The man on the other end said, "Buddy, if I did, I wouldn't be working here." We laugh about it every time we make ravioli, but we don't use brains these days. I have modernized the filling with ground lamb from our ranch and replaced my family's traditional marjoram flavoring with mint. It's much easier to source and just as delicious!

OUR FAMILY'S LAMB RAVIOLI

Makes 8 servings (about 6 dozen ravioli)

First, make the filling: In a large skillet, heat the olive oil over medium heat. Add the onions and cook, stirring occasionally, until they have softened and begin to brown, about 8 minutes. Add the garlic, season with salt and pepper, and cook and stir for another 2 minutes, until super fragrant. Add the spinach a few handfuls at a time, stirring as you go, until all the spinach has been added and starts to wilt. Season again with salt and pepper, then cook for another 5 minutes, or until the spinach is totally wilted and the mixture is dry, lowering the heat as needed if the onions begin to stick to the pan. Transfer the mixture to a plate and set aside to cool for 30 minutes, stirring occasionally to release any steam.

When the mixture has cooled, stir in the lamb, eggs, Parmesan, panko, parsley, and chopped mint, and season with ½ teaspoon salt and ½ teaspoon pepper. (I like to fry up a little patty of the mixture in a pan to taste it for seasoning, then season the mixture more to taste if needed.) Set aside if you will fill the ravioli immediately, or refrigerate for up to 24 hours.

Place one strip of the prepared pasta dough on a large lightly floured work surface. Fill a small bowl with cold water and set it nearby. Fold the dough in half end to end, mark the center of the dough at the fold, and unfold it. Working with only half the dough, use a pastry scraper or the dull side of a large knife to make a long mark lengthwise down the center of the strip of dough, indenting the dough without cutting through it. Next, make crosswise marks (across the dough the short way) at approximately 2½-inch intervals so you have two long rows of approximately 2½-inch squares marked down the entire length of the dough (18 to 20 squares total).

2 tablespoons extra-virgin olive oil

1 medium yellow onion, finely chopped

2 cloves garlic, minced

Kosher salt and freshly ground black pepper

5 ounces baby spinach (about 4 lightly packed cups)

1 pound ground lamb

2 large eggs, beaten

½ cup packed grated Parmesan cheese, plus more for serving

½ cup panko bread crumbs

¼ cup loosely packed finely chopped fresh flat-leaf parsley (leaves and small stems only)

2 tablespoons loosely packed finely chopped fresh mint (leaves and small stems only) plus ½ cup mint leaves, cut into thin ribbons (or left whole if small), for serving

1 recipe Pasta Dough for Homemade Ravioli (page 271), rolled into sheets as directed

1 cup (2 sticks) unsalted butter

Flaky sea salt (optional)

➤

Scoop a scant tablespoon's worth of the lamb filling into your hand, roll it into a ball, and place it in the center of a marked square. Repeat with the remaining squares, keeping the filling as neat and compact as possible, then pat down the filling mounds to flatten them slightly. Dip a few fingers into the water and moisten the dough lightly all around and between the piles and along the dough's edges, dipping your fingers again if necessary. Fold the empty half of the dough over the filling. Using dry fingers, press the long sides of the dough to meet and seal the top and bottom sheets together along the entire length of the dough. Next, press down on the dough around and between each pile of filling, pressing out any air bubbles you can see. (I like to cup my hands and use the rounded pinky sides of my hand to seal right around each mound of filling.) Using a knife or a wavy pasta cutter, cut the mounds into individual ravioli, trimming the long edges of the pasta strip too.

Line a baking sheet with a clean kitchen towel, dust the towel lightly and evenly with flour, and arrange the ravioli on the towel. Dust the ravioli with flour anywhere they seem sticky, and top with another floured kitchen towel.

Repeat with the remaining dough and filling, flouring your work surface before laying down a new strip of dough each time, and stacking the additional ravioli right on top of the first batch as needed in layers, flouring each towel.

When you're ready to cook the ravioli, bring two large pots of salted water to a boil. (You can do this in one pot, but it will take a lot longer to feed everyone!)

Meanwhile, make the browned butter: Melt the butter in a light-colored large, heavy skillet over medium heat. (I use stainless steel or an enameled pan for this so I can see the butter brown as it cooks.) Continue cooking the butter until the solids begin to tan and it begins to smell nutty, about 5 minutes. Remove the pan from the heat and set aside.

Cook about a quarter of the ravioli at a time: Add about 10 ravioli to each pot of water, watch for the ravioli to float to the surface, then cook for 3 minutes, or until the lamb in the center is cooked through, turning all the ravioli once during cooking. Using a slotted spoon or a small strainer, remove the ravioli from both pots, let drain, and transfer to a serving bowl or deep platter with about ¼ cup of the browned butter. Gently toss the ravioli with the butter, top with mint ribbons and Parmesan, shower with a little sea salt, and serve piping hot. Repeat with the remaining ravioli.

You can store uncooked ravioli for up to 24 hours in the fridge, or freeze the ravioli on a baking sheet until firm (in one layer), then transfer them to a ziplock bag and freeze for up to 1 month. Boil the ravioli directly from frozen, adding a minute to the cooking time.

DIY: PASTA DOUGH FOR HOMEMADE RAVIOLI

MY MOM, JANNIE, FREQUENTLY MADE OUR FAMILY'S RAVIOLI RECIPE when my grandparents, Big Jim and Mary (or Marmar), were coming for dinner, often with lots of other family around. Because we made such a large quantity, it was a two-day operation. The first day, my dad would source all the ingredients and my mom would make the filling; the second day, we'd gather around and help roll and form the ravioli. Big Jim always complimented my mom on how it turned out.

My mom bases her pasta recipe loosely on one from Alice Waters's 1984 book *Chez Panisse Pasta, Pizza, and Calzone*. The recipe that follows will serve eight, but you can expand or contract the amounts for your own family. For best results, you'll need a pasta-rolling machine to make the dough sheets; either a hand-crank or stand-mixer-attachment type will work fine.

You can make the dough in advance, but it's best to form the ravioli right after you roll the dough. (You can refrigerate or freeze the uncooked ravioli.)

Makes enough dough for about eighty 2-inch ravioli (8 servings)

On a large, clean work surface, pile the flour in a mound. Add the salt and use your fingers or a fork to distribute it into the flour. Make a well in the center of the flour big enough to hold all the eggs. Crack the eggs into the well, then using a fork, whisk the eggs until uniformly beaten. Slowly increase the stirring circle, incorporating a little flour at a time into the eggs until a dough begins to form. (You can also use your fingers for this.) Continue pulling in flour a little at a time from the edges until the dough is too thick to work with the fork, then switch to your hands and knead the dough, adding flour until the dough no longer sticks to the work surface. (You may not need all the flour. If you add a little too much flour and the dough becomes crumbly, you can sprinkle the dough with water until it comes together.) You should have a somewhat ragged, rough ball of dough. Scrape the work surface clean, dust it lightly with flour, and knead the dough until it's super smooth, about 5 solid minutes of firm kneading (see Note). The dough should feel as soft as the skin on the inside of your forearm. Wrap the dough in plastic and set aside at room temperature for at least 30 minutes and up to 2 hours. (You can also refrigerate the wrapped dough for up to 24 hours.)

4 cups all-purpose flour,
plus more as needed
1 teaspoon kosher salt
6 large eggs
Water

➤→

To roll out the dough, prepare a pasta-rolling machine by lightly flouring the rolling mechanism. Prepare a large work surface or baking sheet by dusting it with flour, and have a stack of clean kitchen towels on hand for covering the rolled dough sheets (which will prevent them from drying out).

Unwrap the dough and cut it into four equal portions. Keep one piece out and cover the rest with the plastic. Flour the dough piece lightly and press one end of it flat so it is thin enough to enter the pasta rollers. With the pasta roller on the widest setting ("1" on many machines), pass the dough through the roller. (If you're using a motor-powered machine, work on the lowest speed.) Fold the dough in half lengthwise, lightly flour the outside, and send it through the machine again on the widest setting. Move to the next-smaller setting ("2" on many machines), lightly flour the dough if it seems sticky, and roll it through the machine. Continue working the dough through the machine on progressively thinner settings, ending with the "6" setting (the thinnest setting on many machines), flouring any sticky spots in the dough as needed. (If the dough sticks, tears, or wrinkles, fold the dough in half once or twice, go back to a thicker setting, lightly flour the dough, and roll it through all the settings again.)

When you're finished, the sheet of dough should be about 5 inches wide (or as wide as the machine) and 4 feet long—and thin enough that when you hold the strip up to the light and put one hand behind it, you can see its shadow through the dough. Lightly flour the entire sheet on both sides, gently fold it into fourths, place it on the floured surface or baking sheet, and cover completely with a clean towel. Repeat with the remaining three dough portions. Once all the dough has been rolled out, it's ready for ravioli.

NOTE: You can also prepare the dough in a stand mixer, mixing the eggs and salt with the paddle attachment on low speed until blended, then switching to the dough hook and gradually adding flour, mixing on low until the dough cleans the sides of the bowl. Knead the dough for 3 minutes on medium speed, until smooth and soft.

If you'd like to use the dough for regular pasta, follow the same instructions, rolling only to a thickness marking of "4" for thin spaghetti or "5" for wider fettuccine. When all four sheets of dough are rolled out, use the machine's cutting attachment to cut the pasta into the desired noodle, or cut the dough into 12-inch lengths, roll the dough sheets up from the short end, and cut them into ribbons with a large, sharp knife. Cook for 3 minutes in well-salted boiling water.

SINCE MAKING RAVIOLI FROM SCRATCH (page 267) is rather time-intensive, I serve a simple custard for dessert that only takes about ten minutes of hands-on time. (I also love it because I usually have eggs, cream, milk, and sugar on hand.) Maisie, always quick with a quip of some sort, claimed this simple egg dessert looked "too boring to be delicious." She took her first bite with a scowl, and then slowly, as the silky-sweet egg melted on her tongue, her entire face lit up. "How is it?" I asked. "I think I've matured into it," she said thoughtfully, nodding. A secret tip from the younger generation? This is also delicious with a little cinnamon sugar sprinkled on top.

FARM-STYLE EGG CUSTARD

Makes 8 servings

Preheat the oven to 350 degrees F. Grease a 7-by-11-inch baking dish (or similar) with butter. Set the dish inside a 9-by-13-inch or larger roasting pan, and place the pans near the oven with a strip of aluminum foil long enough to cover the custard pan.

In a small saucepan, heat the cream and milk over medium heat until the mixture just begins to bubble at the edges. Remove from the heat and set aside to cool for 5 minutes.

In a large mixing bowl, whisk the eggs for about a minute, until thick and foamy. Add the sugar and salt and whisk again to mix, then add the scalded cream in a slow, steady stream, whisking to blend as you go. Tap the bowl on the counter a few times to release any air bubbles.

Pour the custard into the prepared baking dish. Top with the foil, crimping it around the edges to seal, then add boiling water to the roasting pan until it comes about three-quarters of the way up the side of the custard dish. Carefully transfer the pans to the oven and bake for 45 to 55 minutes, or until the custard is set at the edges but still a little jiggly in the center. Remove the pans from the oven. Carefully remove the custard pan from the roasting pan, remove the foil, and cool on a wire rack for 30 minutes. Serve warm, at room temperature, or chilled.

Unsalted butter, for greasing the pan
3 cups heavy cream
1 cup whole milk
8 large eggs
½ cup sugar
Pinch of fine sea salt

THE HEFFERNAN THANKS-GIVING TABLE

Menu for 12

BY THANKSGIVING, FALL ON THE RANCH feels a lot more like winter. Our house sits at 2,775 feet elevation (and the highest point on our hill is 4,300 feet), so we get chilly mountain weather that lasts well into April. When the temperature drops, we start driving up into the 1,400 acres of forest above our barns to gather downed trees, cut them into rounds, and chop them for firewood for the week. Our reliance on wood fires means that gathering wood becomes a crucial part of each weekend.

It may seem like an unnecessary chore in the twenty-first century. My sister, who lives in Nashville, doesn't understand why we don't just have a cord of wood delivered every now and then—or why we don't install modern heating and press a button for warmth! But the answer is simple: We love the dry heat of a wood stove and the comfort it brings, and for us, the process of cutting and stacking wood (and keeping our fire going each day and night) teaches the girls a lot in terms of grit, work ethic, and responsibility. It also makes sense to use the natural resources around us; we live on a mountain with an abundant supply.

Which is all to say that taking a more traditional four-day pause for the Thanksgiving holiday weekend isn't usually in the cards for us. Like most of our community, over Thanksgiving we still spend hours feeding our cattle twice a day and herding the sheep into their barn each evening. We do have a classic Thanksgiving meal, but the food preparation has to fit in and around all the regular chores. We always have a gorgeous turkey, some form of mashed potatoes (Janie's favorite), and a delicious sausage-laden stuffing. My aunt Marge's Jell-O salad (Tessa's favorite) is a must, but the pumpkiny dessert changes every year—it might be a pie, or a cake, or Pumpkin Cheesecake (page 287). Like every other night on the ranch, we feed ourselves only after we've fed the animals. And also like every other night, we give thanks that we can call the ranch home.

MENU TIPS

You can prepare the stuffing and potatoes up to 2 days ahead and cook them after the turkey is done roasting; put the potatoes on the top rack so they brown. To add some greens to the table without taking up precious oven space, serve this feast with Super-Simple Arugula Salad (page 265), Skillet-Grilled Green Beans with Butter and Salt (page 235), or Grilled Zucchini with Garlic Bread Crumbs (page 303)— or a combination of the three!

SINCE THANKSGIVING DAY IS AS BUSY as any other day on the ranch, I don't want to think about making a turkey (beyond defrosting it) until the day I roast it. Luckily it's easy to make a glorious golden turkey without days of brining. I serve mine with a sausage gravy—the browned bits from cooking the sausage add so much to the flavor!—and a jewel-like marmalade made from cranberries and tangy Meyer lemons.

GOLDEN TURKEY WITH SAUSAGE GRAVY AND MEYER LEMON–CRANBERRY MARMALADE

Serves 10 to 12 (with leftovers)

About an hour before you plan to roast the turkey (and 4 hours before you want to serve it), remove the turkey from the fridge and remove any packaging and plastic trussing. Trim off any excess fat and skin, remove and discard any paper and turkey parts inside the bird (or save for another use), and use paper towels to pat the entire bird dry. Transfer the turkey to a baking sheet fitted with a wire rack and let sit at room temperature for 1 hour.

Preheat the oven to 450 degrees F. Arrange a rack near the bottom of the oven and remove any racks toward the top so there's room for the bird.

In a small bowl, stir together the salt, pepper, dried thyme, and lemon zest (reserve the zested lemons for the bird's cavity), stirring or using your fingers to rub the zest into the salt until the zest no longer clumps together. Rub the turkey with the salt mixture inside and out and in all of its cracks and crevices. Tuck the wing tips behind the bird's back. Turn the bird breast side up and stuff the cavity: Halve the reserved lemons and shove them in, along with the garlic, bay, and fresh thyme. Tie the turkey's legs together with kitchen string.

Transfer the bird to a sturdy roasting pan fitted with a roasting rack. Roast the turkey for 30 minutes, then reduce the oven temperature to 350 degrees F, brush the entire bird with the melted butter, and roast for another 30 minutes. At this point, the bird should be good and browned. (If not, delay the aluminum foil step until it is!)

→

FOR THE TURKEY

1 (16- to 18-pound) free-range turkey
2 tablespoons kosher salt
1 tablespoon freshly ground black pepper
2 teaspoons dried thyme
2 Meyer lemons or regular lemons, zested
1 head garlic, halved through its equator
5 dried or fresh bay leaves
1 small bunch fresh thyme
¼ cup (½ stick) unsalted butter, melted
1½ cups dry white wine
1½ cups water

FOR THE GRAVY

Turkey or chicken bone broth, as needed (up to 4 cups)
1 pound mild Italian sausage
¼ cup (½ stick) unsalted butter
⅓ cup all-purpose flour
1 cup heavy cream
Kosher salt and freshly ground black pepper

Meyer Lemon–Cranberry Marmalade (recipe follows), for serving

Cover the turkey lightly with aluminum foil, add the wine and water to the bottom of the roasting pan, and roast for another 1 to 2 hours, or until the meat registers 165 degrees F on an instant-read thermometer inserted in the thickest part of the thigh, the juices run clear when the skin is poked, and the legs wiggle freely. Remove the pan from the oven and gently tip the turkey toward its legs to allow any juices inside the bird to run into the pan. Transfer the bird to a carving board and cover with foil until ready to slice, at least 30 minutes and up to 1 hour.

While the turkey rests, make the gravy: Transfer all the pan juices to a large measuring cup, scraping in any browned bits along with the liquid, and add enough broth to make 4 cups. Set aside.

Heat a large, heavy skillet over medium-high heat. Add the sausage in crumbles all over the pan and cook, stirring only once the sausage releases naturally from the pan and then breaking it up into very small pieces with a spoon or spatula as it continues cooking, stirring until the sausage is well browned and crumbled, about 10 minutes. Scoot it to the edges of the pan and add the butter to the center. When the butter has melted, add the flour and whisk the butter and flour together until thick. While whisking constantly, slowly add the reserved pan juices a little at a time until you've added all the liquid. Simmer for 3 minutes, whisking as the gravy thickens, then add the cream. Season the gravy to taste with salt and pepper and keep warm over very low heat until ready to serve.

Slice the turkey and serve warm with the gravy and marmalade on the side.

Meyer Lemon–Cranberry Marmalade

Makes 2 pints

First, put three small plates in the freezer—you'll use these to test whether the marmalade is ready later.

Trim the ends off the lemons, then quarter them lengthwise and remove as many seeds as you can. Using a small, sharp knife, place a lemon quarter on one flat edge and trim and discard the white pith from the center of the lemon. Cut the wedge crosswise into ⅛-inch-thick slices, removing any additional seeds as you go, and repeat with the remaining lemon quarters. In a large, heavy pot, stir together the sliced lemons and any juice you can collect with the sugar and salt, and let sit for 1 hour (or refrigerate overnight).

Set the pot over high heat and bring the lemon mixture to a boil, stirring frequently, for 5 minutes. Add the cranberries and cook for another 7 to 10 minutes, stirring frequently. (The mixture will foam vigorously and then the foam will subside and the bubbles will get smaller.) After 7 minutes, test the marmalade by dabbing a small blob on a frozen plate for 30 seconds—if it is sticky to the touch and gels enough to not slide down the plate when tipped, it is ready. If not, cook for a minute or two longer and test again.

Transfer the hot marmalade to two pint-size mason jars, cover, and set aside to cool to room temperature. Serve or refrigerate for up to 2 weeks.

NOTE: Since you'll want extra servings of this marmalade for day-after sandwiches (it's also delicious on buttered toast for breakfast), this recipe makes two pints. Double it if you'd like, but make sure to use a pot large enough to accommodate some foaming (or use two pots).

2 pounds (about 7 large) Meyer lemons, well scrubbed
4 cups sugar
Pinch of kosher salt
2 cups fresh cranberries

IF YOU ASK JANIE WHY MASHED POTATOES are her favorite part of Thanksgiving dinner, she says, "Because they're potatoes!" And because potatoes and cheese are basically her two favorite food groups, she goes wild for this crumb-topped cheesy version—and is always ready with the potato peeler. I like them because they're easy to make ahead and also a great side to bring to someone else's house if there's a little extra room in their oven.

JANIE'S CRISPY CHEESY POTATOES

Makes 12 servings

Preheat the oven to 350 degrees F.

Put the potatoes and salt in a large pot with a lid and add enough cold water to cover the potatoes by about an inch. Cover and bring to a boil over high heat, then reduce the heat to low and simmer uncovered until the potatoes are completely tender, 15 to 20 minutes. Drain the potatoes and return them to the pot (off the heat), then mash. Whisk in the milk, then, working with only a few cubes of the chilled butter at a time, whisk in the butter, adding more only when the first batch has melted. Whisk in 1 cup of the cheddar cheese and ½ cup of the Parmesan, then season to taste with salt and pepper. Transfer the potatoes to a 9-by-13-inch baking dish (or similar) and use a spatula to smooth the top.

In a small mixing bowl, stir together the panko and the melted butter until evenly moist, then season with salt and pepper and stir in the remaining 1 cup cheddar and ½ cup Parmesan. Sprinkle the panko mixture evenly over the potatoes. (The potatoes can be made up to this point, covered, and cooled to room temperature. Refrigerate the potatoes until you're ready to cook them, up to 3 days. Add 5 or 10 minutes to the total cooking time if baking straight from the fridge.)

Bake the potatoes for 40 to 45 minutes, or until golden brown on top and piping hot. Serve hot or warm.

4 pounds Yukon Gold potatoes, peeled and cut into 1-inch cubes

1 tablespoon kosher salt

Freshly ground black pepper

1 cup whole milk, at room temperature

¾ cup (1½ sticks) unsalted butter, cubed and chilled, plus ¼ cup melted butter

2 cups (8 ounces) grated sharp cheddar cheese, divided

1 cup (4 ounces) finely grated Parmesan cheese, divided

1½ cups panko bread crumbs

IN MOST HOUSES, I think Thanksgiving might be all about the turkey, but on the ranch, it's all about the pork sausage we've raised—which is why we put it both in the gravy and in the stuffing. Made with leeks, celery, mushrooms, walnuts, cranberries, and plenty of herbs, this stuffing (which is technically a dressing, because it gets cooked outside the bird) could be a one-pan meal in itself. For the best flavor, start with bread that's a day or two old so it soaks up the butter as it gets toasted.

FIVE MARYS SAUSAGE-WALNUT STUFFING

Makes 12 servings

Preheat the oven to 400 degrees F. Line a baking sheet with parchment paper.

Dump the bread cubes on the prepared sheet, drizzle evenly with ½ cup of the melted butter, and toss to coat. Season liberally with salt and pepper, then spread the cubes into an even layer. Bake on the middle rack for about 20 minutes, turning the cubes once or twice, or until golden brown on all sides.

Meanwhile, heat a large, heavy skillet over medium-high heat. Add the sausage, breaking it up, and cook, stirring occasionally and continuing to break it into small pieces, until the meat is cooked through and crisp in spots, about 10 minutes. (If the pork isn't giving up much fat, add a drizzle of olive oil to the pan as it cooks.) Use a slotted spoon to transfer the pork to a large mixing bowl and set aside. Reduce the heat to medium.

Add the leek and celery to the pan with the sausage fat (again, add a swirl of oil if the pan doesn't have a thin sheen of fat across the bottom already), season with salt and pepper, and cook, stirring occasionally, or until the leeks are soft and beginning to take on a little color, about 5 minutes. Add the mushrooms, season again, and cook, stirring frequently, until they shrink considerably, about 5 minutes more. Add the garlic, sage, and thyme and stir for a moment, just until the garlic is fragrant. Transfer the leek mixture to the bowl with the sausage, add the walnuts and cranberries, and stir to incorporate. Add the toasted bread cubes and toss well.

➤——→

1 (2-pound) loaf sourdough, brioche, or challah bread, cut into 1-inch cubes (about 14 cups)

1 cup (2 sticks) unsalted butter, melted, divided, plus more for buttering the pan

Kosher salt and freshly ground black pepper

1 pound Italian sausage (mild or spicy)

Olive oil, as needed

1 large leek (white and light-green parts only), halved lengthwise and thinly sliced (about 2 cups)

2 cups chopped celery (from 5 large stalks)

8 ounces cremini or white button mushrooms, trimmed and sliced

3 large cloves garlic, minced

2 tablespoons chopped fresh sage

1 tablespoon chopped fresh thyme

1½ cups toasted walnuts, roughly chopped

1½ cups fresh cranberries

3 cups turkey, chicken, or beef bone broth

3 large eggs, beaten

FIVE MARYS SAUSAGE-WALNUT STUFFING, CONTINUED

In a separate small mixing bowl, whisk together the remaining ½ cup melted butter, broth, and eggs to blend; season with salt and pepper; and pour the liquid all over the stuffing. Stir until all the bread cubes are moistened, then set the stuffing aside for about 10 minutes to soak up all the liquid, stirring once or twice while it sits.

Butter a 9-by-12-inch or similar pan (or use the same pan you cooked the sausage in, if it's ovenproof and at least 12 inches wide), and pile in the stuffing, pressing down as needed to fit it all into the pan. (You can stop at this point and store the stuffing, covered, at room temperature for up to 1 hour or in the fridge for up to 24 hours.)

Reduce the oven temperature to 350 degrees F and bake the stuffing on the middle rack for 30 minutes, or until golden brown on top. Serve warm or at room temperature. (To make the stuffing ahead, let the stuffing cool to room temperature, then cover with aluminum foil and refrigerate for up to 3 days. To reheat, bake in a 350-degree oven with the foil on for 30 to 45 minutes, or until piping hot.)

BEING A GOOD NEIGHBOR (and having great neighbors) is a big part of our ranching life. Because we all know what it's like when a day on the ranch goes sideways—when our sheep break out of their pen and wander into the road, or when we lose power, or when an animal gets sick—we all know that helping each other is part of our collective responsibility. From small surprise tasks, like helping a neighbor find his dog, to larger yearly chores, like branding and sheep-shearing, we depend on each other. Every time we benefit from the help of others, we try to say thank you—both because it's the right thing to do, and because it's a good example to set for our girls. And nothing says thank you like a good dessert.

Brian and I love cheesecake, so this fluffy pumpkin version is a perfect dessert for us to share with friends on Thanksgiving, to show our appreciation, or to enjoy anytime around the holidays. The hardest part of making it is not eating it immediately. Please be patient; the cheesecake is really best after it has been refrigerated overnight. (You can also make it up to three days in advance.)

PUMPKIN CHEESECAKE

Makes 12 servings

Preheat the oven to 275 degrees F. Grease a 10-inch nonstick springform pan with butter, place on a rimmed baking sheet, and set aside.

To make the crust, put the cookies in the work bowl of a food processor and process until you get fine cookie crumbs. Add the melted butter and confectioners' sugar and pulse until evenly moist. (You can also crush the cookies with a rolling pin in a plastic bag until fine, then mix them with the butter and sugar in a mixing bowl.) Dump the mixture into the prepared pan and pat into an even layer that covers the bottom and goes about ½ inch up the sides.

In the bowl of a stand mixer fitted with the paddle attachment, beat the cream cheese, granulated sugar, and cornstarch together on medium speed for 1 minute, stopping to scrape down the bowl and paddle once halfway through. Add the eggs one at a time, whisking on medium speed between each one just until incorporated. Scrape down the bowl and paddle again. In a separate small mixing bowl, whisk together the pumpkin, vanilla, ginger, nutmeg, cinnamon, cardamom, and salt, then add the pumpkin mixture to the mixer bowl and mix on low speed for about 20 seconds, just until blended, scraping the bowl as needed.

Transfer the mixture to the prepared crust, smooth the top, tap the pan on the baking sheet a few times to release any air bubbles, then bake on the middle rack for 1 hour and 15 minutes, or until the

5 tablespoons unsalted butter, melted, plus more for greasing the pan

9 ounces (about 2 heaping cups) gingersnaps or other hard cookies (such as Biscoff or vanilla wafers)

¼ cup confectioners' sugar

32 ounces regular cream cheese, at room temperature

1 cup granulated sugar

1 tablespoon cornstarch

5 large eggs

1 (15-ounce) can pumpkin puree

1 tablespoon vanilla extract

¾ teaspoon ground ginger

¾ teaspoon ground nutmeg

½ teaspoon ground cinnamon

½ teaspoon ground cardamom

½ teaspoon fine sea salt

cheesecake is set and slightly puffed around the edges but not yet firm in the center. (If you have an oven light, just turn it on to look—it's best not to open the oven door, because temperature swings can cause the cheesecake to crack.) Turn off the oven and let the cheesecake rest for 1 hour in the warm oven. Open the oven door and let the cheesecake sit on the rack, with the door open, for 15 minutes. Remove the cheesecake from the oven and run a butter knife around the edge of the crust to loosen it from the pan. Let it cool to room temperature, then wrap and refrigerate the cheesecake overnight to allow it to firm up. Chill for up to 3 days before serving cold or at room temperature, using a thin-bladed pie server to carefully release the cheesecake from the pan as you cut it.

DIY: BURLAP HOLIDAY TABLE RUNNERS

THE MOST SATISFYING PART about hosting big holiday meals for a crowd is that more people are always welcome—and usually, that means patching together a series of tables that may not necessarily be complementary. Pull them all together visually by making a pretty table runner that covers them all: Start with a length of burlap cloth (which you can buy in long 14-inch-wide rolls at craft stores or online), then simply cut it about 20 inches longer than the table mash-up you want to cover and decorate. Use scissors and your fingers to make a pretty fringe at the short ends, embroider it with simple string, yarn, or thread, then tuck short-stemmed fresh flowers and greenery into the string for a super festive look that doesn't prevent people from being able to see each other. It's much more economical than purchasing something new, especially if you can find pretty greens or small branches on your own property. Top off the decorations with some dried citrus wheels (page 81)—or use your imagination. The runner is just the jumping-off point! The sturdier the greens you choose, the longer the runner will last.

If you're starting with a new roll of burlap, trim off the hemmed end—you want to start with a raw edge before you cut the length of cloth to size so you can make the fringe.

Makes 1 runner

Make a 4-inch cut in from one short edge of the runner, parallel to the length of the burlap and about ¼ inch in from the long edge. Repeat on the other side of the short edge. Using your fingers, loosen and remove the strings of burlap that run the short way across the runner between the two cuts to create a bit of fringe. Continue pulling out and setting aside the crosswise strings, one at a time, until you have 4 inches of fringe on one short end of the runner. Repeat on the opposite end.

Embroider the short edges of the runner: Thread the needle with a 3-foot-long string, position it in the center of the string, and knot the two ends together. Position the runner with a fringed end facing you. Starting on the back side of the runner, poke the needle up through the burlap about ½ inch from where the fringe starts on the right side. Drag the string through the burlap until you reach the knot, then poke the needle back into the burlap from the top about 1 inch to the left of where it came out. Drag the string

- Length of 14-inch-wide burlap from a roll, about 20 inches longer than the table(s) you want it to span
- 1 size-6 quilting needle
- 2 (3-foot-long) pieces white cotton string, yarn, or embroidery thread, plus a few more 6-foot-long pieces as needed, depending on the length of the table
- Fresh flowers and greenery (such as fern, eucalyptus, lemon leaves, evergreen branches, and/or woody herbs like rosemary, sage, and thyme)

➡️

through until it's taut. Repeat, poking the needle up and down through the burlap at 1-inch intervals, moving left as you work until you reach the end, ending with the needle going down. (It will look like a line of dashes.) Tie a knot in the string on the back side of the runner and trim the strings at both ends. Repeat on the other end of the runner.

Using a 6-foot-long string threaded through the needle and tied at the ends, repeat the pattern up the center of the burlap the long way, knotting and starting again with a new piece of string as needed. Center the runner on the table.

No more than 6 hours before you plan to eat, cut the stems on each flower or sprig down to about 4 inches and thread them under the string dashes along the center of the runner. The fresher the flowers (and the closer to serving time you arrange them), the better the arrangement will look far into the night!

———————————————————

NOTE: If you want to make placemats out of burlap with the same design, simply start with short strips of burlap and make the end cuts only about 1 inch long, so you wind up with ¾-inch-long fringe on either side.

ARENA-SIDE DINNER

Menu for 6 to 8

IN MENLO PARK, WHERE I GREW UP, my dad was always the grill guy. He couldn't get enough of standing in front of a hot fire—the bigger the better. He had a regular grill in the backyard, but he really loved cooking for big events, so whenever an opportunity came up, he'd be the one volunteering to tow the school's giant grill to fundraising events and cook tri-tip all afternoon.

After our wedding, when my parents put so much effort into hosting 450 people at their house (on what turned out to be a 108-degree day), we wanted to give my dad a thoughtful thank-you gift, so we commissioned an incredible tow-behind live-fire grill, fashioned just to his liking, down to the cowboy scene crowning the top. It's a Santa Maria–style grill, which means it's equipped with a rotating flywheel that allows the cook to raise and lower the grate—both to add wood and to control how close the food is to the embers. The first few days my dad owned the grill, he parked so he could see it from his car and sat in the passenger seat working on his Blackberry (before working from home was a thing) just so he could glance at it every so often. He was smitten.

But a grill with a cooking surface that's more than three feet deep and six feet wide isn't super practical for two people living in Menlo Park. So a few years later, he drove it up to the ranch and it's been here ever since, parked just outside our little roping arena, where our girls and neighbors practice rodeo at every opportunity. When the weather allows (and often when it doesn't), I prep a mostly grillable dinner in the house while the girls rope. As Brian gets the fire going in the deep pit of the grill, I pile up platters of steaks and veggies a little precariously in the back of my four-wheeler and drive the quarter mile to the arena to grill for the group. While the girls put away the animals and the sun dips below the mountains, the adults gather around the fire pit to keep warm, sipping sidecars, beers, or hot cider. Once the animals have been fed, we dig in.

MENU TIPS

If you're cooking over a live fire a ways from your kitchen, prepare the chermoula butter, bread crumbs, gratin, and pocket pies ahead of time, and do the rest fireside. This menu doubles or triples nicely—just bake the gratin in increasingly larger pans as you scale it up.

OUR ARENA-SIDE DINNERS can be a little tricky in the weather department. In the early fall, the sun is often still strong in the afternoon when the kids are riding, but once it dips below the horizon and our attention turns from roping practice to dinner, things get chilly fast—which is why I like having a warm drink on hand. I sometimes make two pots of this spiced cider (one with booze for the adults and one without for the kids) and keep them on the cooler side of the grill to keep warm (but not boiling) while the rest of the meal is cooking so everyone can have a second serving after dinner.

If you're going to be serving this in legitimately cold weather, warm the mugs first by pouring boiling water in each and letting them sit for a few minutes before emptying them out and filling them with the cider.

HOT GINGER–CRANBERRY CIDER COCKTAIL

Makes 12 cocktails

In a large saucepan, combine the water, cranberries, ginger, maple syrup, cinnamon sticks, and peppercorns and bring to a boil over high heat. Reduce the heat to medium and simmer for 15 minutes, or until all the berries have split open and the liquid is reduced by about half. (If you can, let this mixture sit for at least an hour, or refrigerate and cover for up to 3 days, before continuing.) Add the cider and heat just until steaming—it's important not to boil fresh cider or it will separate—then remove from the heat. Pour 2 tablespoons rum into each of 12 small mugs, then top with cider (with or without the spices).

2 cups water

2 cups fresh cranberries

2 (3-inch) pieces of fresh ginger, peeled and thinly sliced lengthwise

¼ cup good maple syrup

2 cinnamon sticks

1 teaspoon black peppercorns

6 cups (48 ounces) fresh apple cider

1½ cups dark rum or bourbon, divided

THERE'S NO BETTER WAY TO WELCOME FRIENDS to the ranch than with a dinner of grilled steak hot off the coals. For special guests, we'll often break out a big tomahawk steak or a few thick-cut Five Marys rib eyes. But when it's just family, we often choose more economical cuts of beef. Personally, I think sirloin is the most overlooked steak. It has great fat without being overly fatty, and usually has just the right consistency. It's cut thinner than other steaks, so it's quick to cook and difficult to undercook—the perfect steak for people who are intimidated by grilling meat. It's my mom's favorite cut to feed her twelve grandkids; she makes her famous "steak bites" on toothpicks!

Chermoula is traditionally a North African spice-and-herb mixture used on meats, fish, and vegetables. Here, the same flavors are mixed into a butter, which enhances the steak with a lot less work than a fancy sauce. Brian calls this recipe "off-the-rails good," which is pretty much the highest praise he gives. (You know he likes something when he brings a neighbor to the fridge to open, inspect, and taste the leftovers the next day.)

GRILLED STEAKS WITH CHERMOULA BUTTER

Makes 6 to 8 servings

About 30 minutes before grilling, rub the steaks on both sides with the olive oil, season with salt and pepper, and let sit at room temperature until the grill is hot.

Preheat a hardwood fire for grilling (we use oak for the tow-behind grill), or heat a gas or charcoal grill to medium (about 400 degrees F).

To make the butter, in the work bowl of a food processor, pulse the parsley, serrano, garlic, paprika, and cumin until finely chopped, stopping to scrape down the sides of the bowl as needed. Add the softened butter, season with salt and pepper, and pulse and scrape until no visible lumps of plain butter remain. Season to taste, then scrape the butter into a bowl and set aside. (You can also make the butter by finely chopping all the ingredients and mashing the butter into them with a fork. The butter can be made ahead and refrigerated, covered, for up to a week. You can also form the butter into a wrapped log and refrigerate it to be sliced for serving with individual portions.)

➡

FOR THE STEAKS
4 (¾- to 1-pound) sirloin steaks, or 2 (1½- to 2½-pound) rib eyes, or 2 (2½- to 3-pound) tomahawk steaks
2 tablespoons extra-virgin olive oil
Kosher salt and freshly ground black pepper

FOR THE CHERMOULA BUTTER
½ cup roughly chopped fresh flat-leaf parsley leaves and tender stems
1 small serrano pepper (or ½ jalapeño), stemmed and roughly chopped
1 large clove garlic, crushed
¾ teaspoon smoked Spanish paprika
½ teaspoon whole cumin seeds, toasted
6 tablespoons (¾ stick) unsalted butter, cut into pieces, at room temperature
Kosher salt and freshly ground black pepper

When the grill is hot, brush the cooking grates clean. For sirloin steaks, grill for 6 to 8 minutes (with the lid closed), turning once when the steaks are deeply marked by the grill. For rib eyes and tomahawks, grill for 10 to 12 minutes, or until deeply marked, turning once, then move the steaks to the cooler side of the grill and cook for a few more minutes to the desired doneness. (The temperature of sirloin steaks is often hard to measure because they're so thin, but look for the steaks to register 125 degrees F in the center on an instant-read thermometer for medium-rare. A thermometer is especially important for big cuts like tomahawks, for which doneness can be difficult to determine based on appearance.)

Transfer the steaks to a platter, scoop dollops of the butter all over them, cover with aluminum foil, and let rest for 5 minutes. Slice the steaks into ½-inch strips, smearing the butter as you go, and serve warm.

HOW TO SEASON A STEAK

I very rarely season a steak with salt and pepper; most of the time, even when it will be served with a sauce, I use our M5 Spice Rub (see page 21). But whatever you use, seasoning is critical: steak tastes better with salt. I take my steaks out of the fridge to sit at room temperature for about 30 minutes before grilling, which helps them cook more evenly (otherwise, they tend to stay cold in the center). Then I rub them lightly on both sides with olive oil and season them on just one side—that way I can see how seasoned they are.

IN THE FALL, WHEN I'M LOOKING FOR A LITTLE INSPIRATION and the zucchini are still coming in strong, I start topping grilled zucchini with bread crumbs sauteed in butter with anchovies and garlic, which adds crunch and a huge punch of flavor. I love that the bread crumbs are fine at room temperature for a few hours after you make them, and the zucchini cook quickly, so it's a side dish you can pull together in just a few minutes if you do a little prep ahead.

Make as directed, or substitute a teaspoon of finely chopped fresh thyme, rosemary, or sage for the anchovies and add a squeeze of lemon over everything at the end. You can also sprinkle the bread crumbs on almost any grilled veggie; they're great over yellow squash, broccoli, asparagus, and tomatoes—or even Our Family's Lamb Ravioli (page 267) instead of the mint ribbon topping.

GRILLED ZUCCHINI WITH GARLIC BREAD CRUMBS

Makes 6 to 8 servings

Prepare a hardwood fire for grilling, or heat a charcoal or gas grill to medium (about 400 degrees F).

While the grill heats, make the bread crumbs: In a medium saucepan, melt the butter over medium heat. Add the anchovies, garlic, and red pepper flakes, then cook and stir for about 30 seconds, or until the garlic begins to tan. Stir in the bread crumbs, season with salt and pepper, and cook, stirring continuously, until all the bread crumbs are moist and evenly browned, about 2 minutes more. Set aside.

Spread out the zucchini slabs on a baking sheet, brush them on both sides with the olive oil, and season with salt and pepper. Brush the cooking grates clean. Grill the zucchini for 6 to 8 minutes, turning once after about 4 minutes, or until cooked through and well marked on both sides.

Transfer the zucchini to a platter, top with the bread crumbs, and serve immediately.

2 tablespoons unsalted butter

2 jarred anchovies, finely chopped

2 small cloves garlic, minced

¼ teaspoon red pepper flakes

½ cup panko or homemade bread crumbs

Kosher salt and freshly ground black pepper

1½ pounds zucchini (about 3 large), cut lengthwise into ½-inch slabs

2 tablespoons extra-virgin olive oil

NOTE: You can cook the bread crumbs in advance, cool them, and store in the fridge in an airtight container for up to 3 days. In that case, add the crumbs directly to the zucchini after you flip them so the crumbs warm and toast on the grill.

SINCE I ONLY GO TO THE GROCERY STORE every two weeks or so, I stock up big-time on root vegetables. (You know those gigantic bags of russet potatoes available at most grocery stores? I'm the person who buys them, even in the summer.) But it doesn't mean our meals have to be steak-and-potatoes plain, or overly starchy. Take this root vegetable gratin as an example: made with russets, sweet potatoes, turnips, parsnips, and yellow beets, it's a rainbow of vegetables that you peel, slice, stack, and bake into a gorgeous gratin that makes a bold statement on the table but isn't super heavy. It also stays hot for a long time and reheats easily, so it's one of my go-tos when I need to make something ahead and I'm not sure when we'll be having dinner. Adjust the ratio of vegetables however you want—you can also add others, like carrots, rutabaga, or celeriac, as long as the total weight is about 4 pounds and the slices all have roughly the same diameter.

If you'd like, bake this ahead and let it cool to room temperature, then place the dish on the cooler side of a grill to reheat while you cook the rest of your meal.

ROOT VEGETABLE GRATIN

Makes 6 to 8 servings

Preheat the oven to 375 degrees F. Grease an 8-by-11-inch oval gratin dish (or similar) with the butter and set aside.

In a large mixing bowl, toss together all of the potatoes, turnips, parsnips, beets, heavy cream, ⅔ cup of the Parmesan, rosemary, thyme, salt, and pepper. Transfer the mixture to the prepared pan however you see fit—it's lovely to stack the vegetables vertically into the dish a handful at a time, then arrange the stacks in rows or in a spiral. Continue until all the vegetables have been added to the dish, stuffing little pieces in here and there where you can toward the end; it will seem like too many vegetables for the pan, but they will soften and cook down in the oven. Pour any excess cream and herbs over the vegetables and top with the sage leaves. (You can make the gratin up to this point and refrigerate, covered, for up to 1 day. If you do that, add 10 minutes to the first 30-minute baking period.)

Cover the dish with aluminum foil, place on a baking sheet, and bake for 30 minutes. Remove the foil and bake uncovered for 15 more minutes. Top with the remaining ⅓ cup Parmesan and bake for a final 30 minutes, or until the tops of the vegetables are beginning to brown and a toothpick inserted into a stack comes out with no resistance.

Let the gratin cool for 10 minutes, then serve.

1 tablespoon unsalted butter

1½ pounds russet potatoes, ends trimmed, peeled, sliced into ¼-inch-thick discs

1 pound sweet potatoes, ends trimmed, peeled, sliced into ¼-inch-thick discs

½ pound turnips, ends trimmed, peeled, sliced into ¼-inch-thick discs

½ pound parsnips, ends trimmed, peeled, sliced into ¼-inch-thick discs

½ pound yellow beets, ends trimmed, peeled, sliced into ¼-inch-thick discs

1 cup heavy cream

1 heaping cup (about 5 ounces) grated Parmesan cheese, divided

1 tablespoon finely chopped fresh rosemary

2 teaspoons finely chopped fresh thyme

2 teaspoons kosher salt

½ teaspoon freshly ground black pepper

10 small sage leaves

TIM'S GRILLED ONIONS

When you ranch, you learn to rely on neighbors for safety, help, and friendship. We're always happy to lend a hand if anyone's cows get loose, as they'd do for us, but it's the friendship piece that glues our community together. We're pretty much symbiotic with one neighbor family, the Johnsons. Our kids train for rodeo competitions together, and we're always sharing tools or dinner or both at once.

Tim Johnson is a terrific cook who's always ready to take on something new—he makes everything from venison tenderloin to wonton soup. My favorite dish of his is hardly a dish at all, though—it's more of a method, and one that can be done over any sort of fire, any time of year. He wraps onions in aluminum foil and roasts them on a grill (or the outskirts of a fire pit, if he's camping) until they're soft and sweet. They can accompany almost any meal, but are especially great on burgers (page 197) or with ribs (page 159).

To make them yourself, start with 3 or 4 medium onions. Peel them, trimming about ½ inch off the tops but leaving the root ends intact, then cut an X from the top of each onion, slicing about three-quarters of the way through so the root ends hold together uncut. Place a hearty pat of unsalted butter on top of the X, douse with garlic powder and kosher salt (or Tim's favorite, Lawry's Seasoned Salt), and wrap each onion in foil so the ends come up and over the butter. (Tim wraps them in the shape of an onion, with the foiled gathered at the top.) Grill over a medium-heat fire (about 350 degrees F) for an hour or so, or until the onions are completely soft, then move them to a cooler part of the fire until dinner's ready. Serve them in the foil so diners can open them up and eat them with a knife and fork. *(Makes 6 to 8 servings.)*

DIY: HOW TO TETHER A HORSE (OR DOG)

IT CAN BE DANGEROUS for a horse to be tied to something too securely. Because you need to be able to untie them quickly if they get spooked or in case of emergency, it's crucial to use a knot that can be undone in a hurry—and that means a slip knot.

To tether a horse, loop the loose end of its rope over a bar or other solid part of fencing. Pull the loose end to the left of your body, then fold it over the top end of the rope (the part attached to the horse), forming the number 4, with the long line of the number coming from the horse, and the rope forming two short lines in the shape of an L over the long line. The loose end of the rope should be hanging to the right of the rope end closest to the horse. With one hand, hold the two parts of the rope together where they cross. With the other hand, reach into the center of the 4 from the top and grab the loose portion of the rope close to where the lines cross. Pull the rope back up through the center of the 4 (the rope will be doubled over), simultaneously pulling on the horse end of the rope to tighten the knot around the doubled rope and the bar. Some of the loose end of the rope should be hanging free, but when you pull on the horse end, the knot should only tighten.

To untie the knot, pull on the loose end of the rope—the knot will slip free.

ONE YEAR, WHEN TESSA WAS ABOUT SEVEN, we picked up a box of baby chicks at our local post office and brought them home, as we do every so often to replenish our flock. Tessa became enamored with one particular little chick, which she decided to carry around and keep warm in the pocket of her ranch-style pearl-snap shirt as she did her chores. The chick was soon named Pocket, and although she outgrew her temporary home, we still get a family chuckle remembering that little Tessa tried to raise a chicken in her shirt.

Once, when I made these little handheld pies with the girls, we realized they're also pocket-size. We discovered that, using a gentle touch, they could fit the pies into a shirt pocket, mount their horses, and have dessert on horseback. While I don't necessarily recommend transporting them inside your clothing—the deep-red juices of the plum filling will win any laundry-room battle—they're an easy, fun, handheld dessert that kids can take along almost anywhere.

FALL PLUM POCKET PIES

Makes 9 pies

In a small saucepan, stir together the plums, sugar, water, and salt. Bring to a simmer over medium heat and cook for 10 minutes, stirring occasionally, or until the plums have collapsed and given up their juices and the mixture begins to thicken.

Meanwhile, in a small bowl, whisk together the lemon zest and juice and cornstarch. Once the plum mixture is ready, stir in the lemon mixture, return to a simmer (it will thicken a bit more), then pour the filling onto a rimmed plate and transfer to the fridge to cool for 30 minutes.

Gently unfold the puff pastry and discard any paper. On a lightly floured work surface, using a floured rolling pin, roll each of the sheets into 13-inch squares. Lightly flour the sheets, stack as needed, and refrigerate on a parchment-lined baking sheet while the filling cools, about 20 minutes.

When the filling has cooled, arrange one pastry sheet on a work surface. Using the blunt side of a 4-inch round pastry cutter, gently mark 9 circles in the dough, leaving an inch or so of space between each circle. (You're just creating a guide for where to put the filling, not actually cutting through the dough.) Scoop the filling in 2-tablespoon heaps in the center of each marked circle. Using a small pastry brush, gently brush some of the egg wash in a 1-inch swath around each pile of filling. Scoot any filling that strays toward its border back into the center of its circle. (Save the extra egg wash—you'll need it again later.)

1 pound plums (any kind), pitted and chopped into ½-inch pieces
½ cup sugar, plus more for sprinkling the pastry
¼ cup water
¼ teaspoon kosher salt
2 teaspoons lemon zest
1 tablespoon freshly squeezed lemon juice
1 tablespoon cornstarch
2 roughly 9-inch-square sheets puff pastry (from a 17-ounce package), thawed in refrigerator overnight if frozen
All-purpose flour, for rolling out the pastry
1 large egg, beaten

➤

Place the second pastry sheet over the first so the edges match up. Using your fingertips, press the top layer into the bottom layer right around the edge of each pile of filling, doing what you can to ensure there's no air between the layers and no filling escapes. Using the sharp side of the cutter, stamp out each hand pie so you have 9 individual pockets with filling sealed inside. Discard the excess dough, brush away any flour, and use a fork to crimp all the way around the edges of each pie. Gently transfer the pies back to the baking sheet and refrigerate for at least 30 minutes and up to 4 hours.

Preheat the oven to 400 degrees F. Brush the pastries with egg wash and shower them with sugar. Using a small, sharp knife, cut three ¾-inch or so vents in the top of each pie, then bake for 20 minutes, or until they are nicely puffed and browned. Let cool for about 15 minutes on the pan, then serve warm or at room temperature. Store any uneaten pies in a sealed container at room temperature for up to 2 days.

Anytime Menus for Six

PREP-AHEAD CELEBRATION DINNER

Saltine-Crusted Bite-Size Crab Cakes with Jalapeño Tartar Sauce (page 67)

Long Day Manhattans (page 252)

Grilled Steaks with Chermoula Butter (page 299)

Icebox Pull-Apart Rolls (page 53)

Root Vegetable Gratin (page 304)

Skillet-Grilled Green Beans with Butter and Salt (page 235)

Farm-Style Egg Custard (page 273)

SUMMER-ON-THE-GRILL DINNER

Cumin-Coriander Spareribs with Honey Barbecue Sauce (page 159)

Grilled Zucchini with Garlic Bread Crumbs (page 303)

Campfire Peaches with Sourdough Streusel and Brown Sugar–Vanilla
  Ice Cream (page 186)

LET THE KIDS MAKE DINNER

Walk-Away Pot Roast with Mashed Sweet Potatoes (page 51)

Perfect Wild Rice (page 257)

Rhubarb Clafoutis (page 96)

ONE-AND-DONE DINNERS

One-Pan Spicy Meatball Bake (page 18)

Sheet-Pan Pork Tenderloin with Delicata, Kale, and Brussels Sprouts (page 255)

Our Favorite Sausage Stew with Grilled Bread (page 182)

Lamb and Root Vegetable Potpie with Leaf Lard Biscuit Crust (page 35)

Double-Beef Chili with Black Beans and Sweet Potatoes (page 131)

Acknowledgments

NO PROJECT ON THE RANCH happens without help—and *Five Marys Family Style* was no exception. While this book's recipes and stories are rooted in my family's traditions, I also had a whole "cookbook family" helping to bring this project to life.

Thanks to Jess Thomson, my recipe developer and coauthor. Jess was my compass and right-hand gal in this process from start to finish, leading the charge but also keeping us sane as we worked through each menu concept, and becoming a great friend in the process. Jess, "your room" in the guesthouse is always open and my kitchen is your kitchen now!

Thanks, as always, to my amazing agent, Leslie Stoker, for helping me navigate the cookbook-producing process yet again from beginning to end. Leslie, your judgment and insights are always exactly what I need at just the right moment.

Thanks to Erin Kunkel, this book's gifted photographer, who (with her trusty pup, Billie, and husband, Danny) put so much effort, talent, and imagination into the photos she took over the course of almost two years. She connected with my girls over horses and rodeo, and gave them each the attention they deserved here. Thanks also to food stylists Abby Stolfo, Veronica Laramie, and Allison Fellion, and prop stylist Kaeja Korty, for their expertise, creativity, and patience throughout every long day of our photo shoots. Also thanks to my local go-to gal for Scott Valley photography, Della Hayden, who captures our beautiful corner of the world in any weather.

Thanks to the publishing team at Sasquatch Books, especially Susan Roxborough, who helped guide this book's concept and content from the very start. Huge thanks to the rest of the crew too: art director Anna Goldstein, marketing director Nikki Sprinkle, VP of sales and strategy Jenny Abrami, editor Jill Saginario, copyeditor Rachelle Longé McGhee, and publicist Molly Woolbright. It was a pleasure.

Thanks to my lovely, supportive community here in Fort Jones, California. From the staff and customers in my shop and at our restaurant to the neighbors who inspire us to live life to its fullest, I appreciate the village that contributes new recipes to our family traditions. (Johnson family, I'm looking at you.)

Finally, a huge thanks to my family. First, to my parents, Janet and John, who showed me what it means to eat well and entertain (and also hosted us for a photo shoot). You make life so fun and delicious, and I'm so grateful I can pass that spirit on to our four Marys. To Brian and the girls: thank you for showing such patience not only during the photography for this project, but also during many late nights and emergency meetings, and all the other unseen dramas involved in getting any book to print. You are always my inspiration to keep creating, and none of this would be possible without you.

Index

Note: Page numbers in *italic* refer to photographs.

About the Author

MARY HEFFERNAN and her husband, Brian, left behind the busy life they'd built in Silicon Valley to become cattle ranchers with their four young daughters—all named Mary. Together they own and operate Five Marys Farms, a 1,800-acre ranch in the mountains of Northern California, where they live, work, and raise all-natural beef, pork, and lamb. Mary and Brian sell and ship directly from the farm to families all over the US through their Farm Store in Fort Jones. They share their meats with local customers and visitors from far and wide at their popular restaurant and bar, Five Marys Burgerhouse. Five Marys was awarded Best Farm in America by *Paleo* magazine and has been featured in *Oprah* magazine, *Real Simple*, *Sunset*, and other national publications. Mary has also appeared on *Today*. She has a fiercely loyal following on social media and hosts popular summer farm dinners and weekend retreats at the ranch with cooking, cocktails, and butchery classes. She and Brian believe in raising meat naturally and that great cooking starts with well-raised ingredients. For more information on Five Marys Farms, and to order meat, visit FiveMarysFarms.com.

Contributors

JESS THOMSON is an award-winning freelance food and travel writer, and the author of eleven cookbooks, some cowritten with nationally acclaimed restaurateurs and influencers, plus her memoir, *A Year Right Here: Adventures with Food and Family in the Great Nearby*. Her work has appeared in the *New York Times* (where she is a regular recipe tester), *Food & Wine*, *Cooking Light*, *Seattle*, *Sunset*, and *Edible Seattle* magazines, and in multiple issues of the yearly *Best Food Writing* book collection. Jess also does corporate recipe development and testing, focusing on recipes for product launches. She lives in Seattle with her husband and thirteen-year-old son.

ERIN KUNKEL is an award-winning food and lifestyle photographer who has traveled around the world and is always up for an adventure. When she's not behind the camera, she's usually cooking, gardening, surfing, road tripping with her pup, Billie, and husband, Danny, or fixing up their getaway cabin in the Santa Cruz mountains.

Printed in China

SASQUATCH BOOKS with colophon is a registered trademark of Penguin Random House LLC

26 25 24 23 22   9 8 7 6 5 4 3 2 1

Photographer: Erin Kunkel
Additional photographs: Della Hayden, pages 8–10, 14, 32, 48, and 326
Editors: Susan Roxborough and Jill Saginario
Designer: Anna Goldstein
Food stylists: Abby Stolfo, Veronica Laramie, and Allison Fellion
Prop stylist: Kaeja Korty

Library of Congress Cataloging-in-Publication Data
Names: Heffernan, Mary, 1978- author. | Thomson, Jess, author.
Title: Five Marys family style : recipes and traditions from the ranch / Mary Heffernan with Jess Thomson.
Description: Seattle, WA : Sasquatch Books, [2022] | Includes index. |
Identifiers: LCCN 2021042310 (print) | LCCN 2021042311 (ebook) | ISBN 9781632174024 (hardcover) | ISBN 9781632174031 (ebook)
Subjects: LCSH: Seasonal cooking. | Ranch life—California. | LCGFT: Cookbooks.
Classification: LCC TX714 .H4345 2022 (print) | LCC TX714 (ebook) | DDC 641.5/64—dc23
LC record available at https://lccn.loc.gov/2021042310
LC ebook record available at https://lccn.loc.gov/2021042311

ISBN: 978-1-63217-402-4

Sasquatch Books | 1325 Fourth Avenue, Suite 1025 | Seattle, WA 98101

SasquatchBooks.com

MIX
Paper from responsible sources
FSC® C001701

Conversions

VOLUME			LENGTH		WEIGHT	
UNITED STATES	METRIC	IMPERIAL	UNITED STATES	METRIC	AVOIRDUPOIS	METRIC
¼ tsp.	1.25 mL		⅛ in.	3 mm	¼ oz.	7 g
½ tsp.	2.5 mL		¼ in.	6 mm	½ oz.	15 g
1 tsp.	5 mL		½ in.	1.25 cm	1 oz.	30 g
½ Tbsp.	7.5 mL		1 in.	2.5 cm	2 oz.	60 g
1 Tbsp.	15 mL		1 ft.	30 cm	3 oz.	90 g
⅛ c.	30 mL	1 fl. oz.			4 oz.	115 g
¼ c.	60 mL	2 fl. oz.			5 oz.	150 g
⅓ c.	80 mL	2.5 fl. oz.			6 oz.	175 g
½ c.	125 mL	4 fl. oz.			7 oz.	200 g
1 c.	250 mL	8 fl. oz.			8 oz. (½ lb.)	225 g
2 c. (1 pt.)	500 mL	16 fl. oz.			9 oz.	250 g
1 qt.	1 L	32 fl. oz.			10 oz.	300 g

TEMPERATURE				WEIGHT (cont.)	
OVEN MARK	FAHRENHEIT	CELSIUS	GAS	11 oz.	325 g
Very cool	250–275	130–140	½–1	12 oz.	350 g
Cool	300	150	2	13 oz.	375 g
Warm	325	165	3	14 oz.	400 g
Moderate	350	175	4	15 oz.	425 g
Moderately hot	375	190	5	16 oz. (1 lb.)	450 g
Fairly hot	400	200	6	1½ lb.	750 g
Hot	425	220	7	2 lb.	900 g
Very hot	450	230	8	2¼ lb.	1 kg
Very hot	475	245	9	3 lb.	1.4 kg
				4 lb.	1.8 kg